Polymer Clay Gemstones

The Art of Deception

Kim Schlinke & Randee M. Ketzel

Polymer Clay Gemstones—The Art of Deception

Photography by Ricardo Acevedo
and Randee M. Ketzel
Book design by Sarajane Helm

First published and printed as a paperback in
the United States of America 2013
by PolyMarket Press

ISBN 978-0-9800312-9-4

POLYMARKET PRESS

For more information about our books
and the authors and artists who create them,
please visit our website:
polymarketpress.net

Acknowledgments

Every artist working in polymer clay today who delights in the marvelous capacity of this medium to mimic other materials owes an enormous debt to both Tory Hughes and Irene S. Dean—two of the great pioneers of faux technique. Their work inspired much of the material herein, and we hope we have done justice to their efforts in promoting the most exciting art medium on the planet. We also give grateful thanks to the ever-creative Donna Kato, (for just about everything) and to Linda Geer, for suggesting the materials for ammolite. Beyond these, the whole of the polymer community who so generously share ideas and techniques—you know who you are.

None of this would have been possible without the guidance and generosity of Polymarket Press, in particular Sarajane Helm.

This book never would have been more than a twinkle in our eyes without our wonderful supportive families, who cooked and cleaned for themselves without lasting damage.

Lastly, we owe thanks to our local guild, a creative assembly of people who inspire and support the polymer arts. If you don't belong to a guild, find and join one!

The narrative contained herein is a work of fiction, though the town of Waterloo does exist, known today as Austin, TX. The situations and characters portrayed are products of our imagination; any resemblance between them and any actual persons living or dead are the products of *your* imagination.

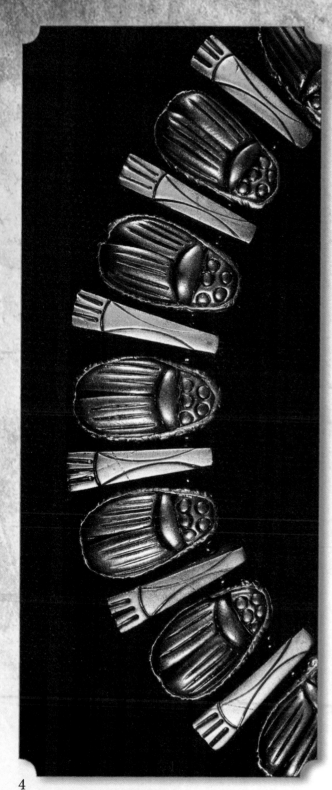

Contents

the Case of the Fantastical Forgeries

"I am desperately bored, Parker..." declared Miss Zylphia Peele, putting a theatrical hand to her brow, "so bored, I am seriously thinking of doing my taxes...on time."

Noelia Parker heaved a patient sigh. "Now, Peele," her companion returned soothingly, "how can you say that? What with those mysterious sightings in Zilker Park, right here in the heart of Waterloo?"

"Waterloo is a dull backwater," began her friend.

"Nonsense!" declared Parker, "Stuff and nonsense! The most preeminent city in the Republic—why, people still remember when Comanche braves were raging down this very street."

Peele waved a dismissive hand. "That is no recommendation for tourists, and so far as those 'mysterious' sightings—really, Noelia; arboreal ghosts? Albino squirrels, however monstrous, are hardly a matter for my talents." Peele moved to the window of their lodgings, high above Pecan Street in the Driskill Hotel. She pulled aside the curtain and surveyed the scene below, "Cattle, Parker, going about their daily forage."

Parker shook her paper vigorously. "I say, Peele," determined to ignore her companion's foul mood,

"That author, Porter—the one with those devilish clever stories—will be reading at Maggie Mae's tonight; care to go?"

"Faugh!" sniffed Peele. "Maggie Mae's? In late September, overrun with lads who really should be back at school."

Parker sniffed back: "Sorry, thought it might amuse you."

"So," she pursued after a long pause, "what do you want to do tonight?" With no reply forthcoming, she turned to observe her longtime companion peering through her opera glass at the street below.

"I do believe the day just became more interesting," Peele murmured.

A few moments later a chime sounded at their door and Parker answered it. "Beg pardon, Miss," said the grizzled doorman, pulling his forelock. "A gentleman 'ere to see Miss Peele."

Parker carried the proffered card to her flat-mate, who tossed it back onto the tray with an amused glance. "Have Nelson bring him up," she said, "and some tea as well." Peele turned to the bookcase and riffled through her personal file, pulling out a card. "Pother, Leslie," she announced, "for ten months head curator of the Waterloo Natural History Museum."

The chime announced both guest and tea. Parker tipped the doorman and dismissed him, murmuring, "Do get a decent haircut...always on my mind." She ushered their guest in and bade him take a seat, from which he hastily bobbed up as Peele entered. She graciously waved him back and took the one opposite.

"Mr. Pother, we are delighted to have your company this afternoon—all is well at the museum, I take it?"

Pother opened and shut his mouth, blinking; then stammered, "Yes, thank you, well...no, not precisely, I mean to say, at least nothing's gone missing...oh!" He wailed, throwing up his hands; "I've no idea how to begin..."

Peele settled deeper into the armchair and steepled her hands. "I find it's best to begin at the beginning, then go on until you reach the end." She tilted her head back and composed herself. "I cannot make tea without water, sir."

Mr. Pother fidgeted nervously. "I must ask that you

breathe no word of this to anyone."

Peele raised a stern eyebrow. "No one for whom I have investigated a matter has ever had cause to complain of my discretion, sir." He rolled a flighty eye in the direction of Miss Parker. "Or that of Miss Parker."

"Well!" bleated Pother, wringing his hands. "It happened last night; as he was making his rounds of the Gems and Minerals wing, one of our watchmen heard a sound. Turning the corner, he surprised a burglar in the act of prising open a wall case. When he shouted an alarm, the burglar charged straight into him, knocking him down, and by the time the fellow recovered his wits, the ruffian had vanished. When help arrived, it was discovered that theft had been narrowly averted—

7

the case was damaged, but the contents were intact."

Peele closed her eyes and waved an impatient hand. "What more?"

Mr Pother picked up his cup and swallowed it at a gulp. "Of course I came round at once, and proceeded to remove the contents of the case for safe-keeping—it's an extremely valuable collection, you see—"

Peele raised a finger, "Mr. Pother, did your watchman describe the man; assuming that it was a man?"

Pother blinked furiously and his Adam's apple bobbed up and down in an alarming manner. "I...why, I never thought of that. The watchman only described an uncommon short and solid creature—said it was like being hit by a boulder—but there was something odd."

Peele opened one eye. "Yes?" Pother's ears assumed a pinkish tinge.

"He, mmm, mentioned that the burglar had...a rather distinct aroma."

Peele smiled contentedly. "We'll get back to that; let's hear the worst part."

"How did you..?" whispered Pother as he mopped his brow. He resumed. "In the process of removing the items from the case, one slipped from my fingers. The article in question was a Qin dynasty jade bangle—a lovely example of its kind; it fell to the floor before I could catch it," he took a deep breath, "where it landed with a dull thud." Peele's other eye flew open and she regarded the quivering man.

"Burmese jadeite" she said, "rings like a bell when it strikes a hard surface."

"Quite," said Pother, in a strangled voice. "So, of course I took it and every article from the case, and submitted them to our staff experts for examination—and the results were unequivocal: Every single artifact, all from one private collection, were extremely clever forgeries."

Peele rubbed her chin thoughtfully, "How could they have passed muster at the time of admission?"

"Ah," replied Pother unhappily, "therein lies the rub—they were admitted to the museum under the tenure of my predecessor, and there is no record that they were ever subjected to any scrutiny before being put into inventory."

"That," declared Peele, is highly unusual, unless..."

"Yes." whispered Pother, "Quite. Unless the donor is of so stainless a character that the usual protocols are waived."

Peele winked at her companion. "Stand by for an illustrious name, Parker; please, Mr. Pother—spare us the cruel suspense. Who is this donor of this mysterious brummagem?"

Pother closed his eyes miserably, "That is the heart of a very delicate problem; the donor is Baron Gaylord du Vane—the Lord Mayor himself."

A wicked grin spread across Zylphia Peele's lips. "Fetch your reticule, Parker. I feel an expedition coming on."

In the shadowy halls of the Natural History Museum, a breathless audience watched as Miss Peele stood in rapt concentration of the crime scene. She slowly turned and paced in different directions, eyes closed, then all at once threw herself headlong upon the floor to lie prone, looking glass at the ready.

She withdrew a pair of silver tweezers from her pocket and used them to secure a tiny black clod. "Observe," she said, waving the specimen beneath her companion's nose, "this came from the shoe of our incompetent robber. What do you deduce?"

Parker sighed heavily. "Well, it's dirt, Peele."

"Wrong! As always, dear girl, you see, but...oh well." Peele sniffed the specimen thoroughly, then without ceremony popped it into her mouth, chewed vigorously, and swallowed it at a gulp. She looked round. "I have tasted all 802 varieties of dirt extant in the Waterloo area; this is not one of them. It is in fact the excreta of Tadarida brasiliensis; or as you know it..."

She went silent, ignoring the shocked expressions of her audience. "But, of course, one must not form conclusions without corroborating evidence." Without another word she set off down the corridor in the direction of the entrance, Parker hurrying in her wake.

A short time later, both were being ushered through the marble halls of Folie De Grandeur, the resplendent town house of the Baron Du Vane, Lord Mayor of Waterloo. This worthy received them in his library with sherry and biscuits. "Now, ladies," began the Mayor, smoothing his hair and treating both women to his election-year smile, "to what do I owe the honor of this visit?"

Miss Peele sipped her sherry. "Lord Mayor, I believe you have heard of the attempted robbery of the Waterloo Museum this morning? Because it was directed at the case containing the collection you so generously donated to the museum last year, we are anxious to know the history of these items—their provenance. Were they family treasures? Or acquired on your travels?"

"Tut!" replied the Lord Mayor, "None of the above. They were acquired here in Waterloo a few years ago. I had the entire collection from a lady…"

"Indeed," tittered the Miss Parker, who then collected herself, "pray, go on; does the lady have a name?"

"Oh," said the Baron, waving a negligent hand, "of course she must, but I don't recall it. She begged the favor of a meeting one evening saying that it would be to my advantage, and so it was."

"Might you be able to describe the lady?" asked Peele.

The Lord Mayor pursed his lips and scratched his head absently, disarranging the comb-over to reveal a shiny expanse of scalp. "Well," he began, "it was a deuced dark—she insisted upon meeting at foot of the Congress Avenue Bridge—you know the place, I am certain. Let me see: a solid specimen, taller than is common, with largish, very worn hands; wore a dark hat, veils;" he brightened suddenly. "I can tell you though, she wore a magnificent mourning brooch—wouldn't part with it, though it nearly queered the deal."

"Very good," said Peele soothingly; "a widow, I take it?"

"Oh quite," said the Baron, warming to his subject, "gave out she was in dire need of funds, and must part with her family treasures. Knowing my reputation as a collector, she sought an interview."

"Tsk," said Peele wisely, "Widows…no doubt she played upon your sympathy to wheedle an exorbitant price?"

" Ha!" crowed Du Vane. "Am I such a greenhorn? Of course she tried! Whined and sniveled about pensions and cat food, but I bargained sharp, I can tell you—ended up getting the lot for the price of a meal at_____." Here the Lord Mayor named the best Mexican restaurant in Waterloo. He grinned and thumped his chest, "Sell dear and buy cheap, is my motto."

"Quite." murmured Peele, setting her sherry down carefully. "And why, pray tell, did you value the collection at twenty times that price when you donated it to the Museum?"

The Baron flushed scarlet and was seized with a fit of coughing; he sputtered indignantly behind his handkerchief. "Who the h___ spilled the beans?!"

"No one," returned Peele, standing up and pulling on her gloves. "It is conjecture, based upon my knowledge of your character. Good afternoon, Lord Mayor; we'll see ourselves out."

As the great iron gates clanged behind them, Parker raised an eyebrow and said "He's a warm man, the Baron; cheating widows, no less...or thought he was."

"Exactly," returned Peele, "and his boasting assures me that he knew nothing of their nature; regarded it rather as a feather in his cap. We must look farther for the source of the deception. At least the curator will be relieved to know that he need not clap the Lord Mayor in irons for a taradiddle, though of course the tax authorities may have a different view. We must to the Congress Avenue Bridge, Parker. Both threads of the investigation are leading us there."

Mid-afternoon found the detective and her faithful companion braving the muddy trail which led beneath the old bridge. Parker had her handkerchief to her nose exclaiming "What the devil is that stench, Peele?!"

Her companion laughed, "I should say upwards of two million Mexican Freetail bats. They live in the cracks of the bridge above us." Parker cast a fearful eye upwards. "Don't do that," murmured Peele "nor open your mouth, there's a wise gel."

Parker stared ruefully at the great dark mounds before them. "That is what I think it is, isn't it?" she queried.

"Indeed," replied Peele cheerfully, "fuel, fertilizer and a dandy source of explosives. Useful little animal, the bat. Eats its weight in noxious insects every night."

"And certainly keeps the ground moist," grumped Parker, shaking off her sleeves.

As they descended into the foetor, Peele wondered aloud, "Why here, Parker?"

Her companion responded with a chuckle, "Grade school, dear girl, grade school! Both the avarice of Baron DuVane and the sample on the floor of the museum indicate that this is the place."

"What?!" sputtered Parker "You mean that clod you ingested...?"

"Parker," reproved Peele, "one must investigate thoroughly."

They clambered over the soft mounds of refuse, waving their arms to fend off the curious creatures who swooped down by ones and twos to investigate—insomniacs, obviously—when all at once, the hummock they were approaching exploded in a flurry of odoriferous dust.

"OY!" cried the mound of dirt. "Oo're you, then?!" Parker stepped back in alarm as Peele laid her hand on the hilt of her umbrella.

What appeared to be a shapeless lump of guano, ticking, and oddments of garbage resolved itself into a roughly human appearance, though a human of exceedingly short and shapeless mien. As it raised a greasy face to the faint light, it was apparently female, but that was as far as either of the intrepid investigators was willing to vouchsafe. The creature trundled forward, crying "Please Miss, there's a nice laidy—we've not eaten in a fortnight—please mum, a bit of something—"

"Here, here," cried Parker, backing hastily away from the noisesome pawing, "I'll see if I have something; give us a moment—"

"Hold there!" called Peele sharply, and the varmint froze on the instant, blinking up at the detective. "What are you called, Madame?"

"Ooo, miss, we're Bumm, Odia Bumm, as is...please miss, a copper or two...just a copper?"

"Miss Bumm," said Peele firmly, "you dwell here, do you not?"

The tramp cackled, "Me? Me, dwelling? O, aye, this is me dwelling—me office too, as ye likes."

"Yes," returned Peele icily, "and your trade is all too apparent. Parker, be so good as to check your reticule." Parker clapped her hand to her waist, only to find the article no longer in its accustomed place. She turned indignantly to the lumpish beggar, backing away. Just as Peele moved to block the creature's escape, it raised its head and uttered a bloodcurdling shriek; Peele hooked the thief's robe with her umbrella handle as thousands upon thousands of bats descended upon them in a dark and panicked cloud. The two detectives took shelter beneath the umbrella to escape the sharp wings and claws of the tiny creatures. After a few moments, the alarm was over. Peele and Parker stood to watch the last of the furry tribe wing off into the gloaming.

"That was exceedingly interesting," observed Peele.

"Interesting!?! Interesting!! Peele, do you realize that filthy beast robbed me?!"

"Calm yourself, my dear girl," answered Peele, "here are your things, and a few others." Peele held up a grimy sack, from which tumbled Parker's silk reticule, a man's wallet and several watches, as well as a small wooden case. "This was inside her cloak," explained Peele, "of which I divested her before she could abscond completely."

Parker scooped up her belongings with relief. "But where in the devil has she gone? And how could a crippled oaf like that move with such speed?"

"Ah." said Peele, laying a finger aside her nose. "Things are seldom what they seem; and this blinking idiot is a case in point. I wouldn't be at all surprised if she were far more resourceful than she appears—certainly, we need look no farther for the maker of last night's mischief. The odor that the guard reported? It was eau de Bumm. The tracks lead this way, Parker."

It was growing dark as the twain made their way through the piles of dung. Peele pulled out her torch and shone it on the soft ground, following the beggar's flight. The tracks stopped at the base of one of the massive stone piers supporting the bridge, where they milled in confusion and the trail disappeared.

Parker turned to her friend in confusion, "What the devil? Did she run slap into the wall and disappear?"

Peele shook her head as she sorted through the beggar's pouch. "Not at all, Nosie," ignoring her friend's squirm at the use of her old school name, "she's around here somewhere, I daresay—could be that pile of garbage over there. But the reason she ran here was to get to her refuge, for whose door, unhappily, she had lost her key." Peele opened the wooden case which had been amongst the swag and extracted a large bronze key. "Let's see where we can stick this." A few moments of close examination of the rock face revealed little, until Parker bent down to brush an insect off her shoe. "Ha," uttered Peele softly, "there." Barely an ell off the ground, marks of grimy fingers were just visible. Peele picked at them gently until a flake of stone dislodged itself from a man-made opening. Peele inserted the key and turned it with a snap. With a low hiss, a section of the wall swung open, revealing a staircase leading down into darkness. "Age before beauty," murmured Peele, gesturing to her friend.

"Pearls before swine," retorted Parker, seizing the torch. As the intrepid duo reached the foot of the stairs, lights triggered by some unseen mechanism flickered and then illuminated a damp and cavernous room.

"Well,well," said Peele, rubbing her hands together with glee, "Ali Baba's cave, indeed." The room was furnished as an artist's studio, with orderly racks of supplies and tools. Worktables were covered with colorful lumps of strange material, and gleaming silver machines like those in the best Italian kitchens stood silent guard.

"What is this stuff?" wondered Parker, and her companion pointed her umbrella to the drawings that plastered the walls.

"The raw materials for the best forgeries ever seen" replied her friend. "This is where they were created." Together they examined the drawings, exclaiming softly as they recognized several objects from the Museum.

Parker picked up one of the colorful lumps and frowned. "What is this, Peele? It's soft like clay, but I've never seen these colors before."

"No," said her friend, "nor have I—at least in this form. I suspect it requires a catalyst of some type to render it into the false gems—ah, here!" Peele uncovered an array of electric ovens. "Heat—how charming. This must be some type of polymer, which, when brought to the proper temperature, then hardens. I have heard rumors. Could become just about anything, in skilled hands."

"Those hands were obviously here," said Parker, as she made her way over to an easel which held a large map of Waterloo.

"Two pairs, if I'm not mistaken," agreed Peele, measuring the height of the chair seats with her umbrella. "One tall, one average. A pretty pair of criminal genii."

As Parker picked up a sketch from a nearby table, she surprised an enormous palmetto bug; her precipitous leap brought her hard up against a bookcase, from which a cache of slender volumes cascaded down. Peele picked one up and scanned it rapidly. "If you can't stand the heat—stay away from the cookbooks," she quipped. She loaded them into Parker's arms, and glanced about the room, "We'll have the gendarmes set a watch, but for now, let us repair to our lodgings and examine the booty." She ignored the grumbles of her laden companion. "Come along, Parker; don't dawdle."

~Sometime Later~
"These are really fascinating," said Parker, leafing through the volume in her lap, "Imagine; creating a thousand year old cycladic figure in stone so realistic it fools the eye."

"Indeed," returned Peele, similarly engrossed in her own pamphlet. "Every step in construction has been detailed—these forgers are the paragons of polymer. Look, there's even a primer for her apprentice, lest she should forget a basic step. So methodical...and every secret of their minds is now open to us; one the master, the other the student; let's see how they accomplished it."

At that moment, a chime sounded. Peele looked up in irritation, "Expecting anyone, Noelia?"

Parker answered by going to the door and opening it, only to discover an empty corridor. She retrieved an envelope from the threshold, "Addressed to you, Peele."

Miss Peele slit the envelope open and began to read:

"My Dear Detective—or is that how you style yourself? I should say it was unbecoming of a lady to indulge in such pursuits, were I not myself similarly inclined. Where our avocations diverge is in the object; you seek the truth. I seek to confound it. Both are arts—one which I prosecute with a single-minded intent.

I am the hand behind the best forgeries of ancient jewelry ever created; and you have been privileged to witness my first essays. You may assume my motive is pecuniary—and you are wrong. It is the art of the game alone which draws me. I sent my henchwoman Bumm to the museum to retrieve that of which the Baron so foolishly imagined he had swindled me; having passed their test, they needed to disappear so that I might be free to realize the next stage of my work. A failure of execution; her last.

The wretched Bumm was apprehended earlier this evening on an anonymous tip—I do so despise incompetence—but rest assured that the questioning of the police will only yield up a name you know all too well, that of your companion, Nosie Parker. Oh dear, it's really Noelia, isn't it? Perhaps a bit cold of me, after so many years as my cat's paw, but one should never be sentimental when dealing with criminals.

Do not imagine that you have caused me anything more than momentary inconvenience; soon I will have completed the construction of my second atelier, and there I will create masterpieces of the forger's art, undetectable even by the sharpest scrutiny. You will forever wonder, walking through museums or attending grand balls, if the jewels you are admiring are the products of my genius.

As for your success in tracking me down, I wish you none; nor am I in the least apprehensive. You will never discover my name, nor that of my faithful apprentice...

But dear me, perhaps you already know it? Perhaps I am someone you pass in the street every day—the charwoman at the hotel, or the cook at your favorite restaurant; perhaps.

Au revoir, Peele; content yourself with solving the little mysteries Waterloo has to offer—the stray tomcats two and four legged; but waste not another moment of your time in pursuit of me, for I am a quarry entirely beyond your ken and abilities."

Peele pulled in an angry breath, and Parker watched apprehensively, knowing what it took to arouse her companion to that state. But when she looked up, Peele wore a wry smile. "At least we're confirmed it's a woman," she said, "and much given to hubris; a fault which we may use to the good."

She paced over to the darkened window and peered out. "Probably watching from the street this very moment." She gave a mocking salute to the night.

Parker sat down quietly. "And what now?" she asked.

Peele shook her sleeves vigorously. "Always use what you have in hand, Parker; and we have these."

She turned to the stack of handwritten folios which were piled upon the table. "Our forger has poured her heart and soul into these instruction manuals. Somewhere here are the clues to identifying her. We'll take them one by one—in fact at first light, we'll repair to the underground lair, and reconstruct each piece. In that process, we'll bell this mysterious cat. To bed, Nosie! We have some long and interesting days ahead of us, starting tomorrow."

Parker rose and headed for her chamber, then looked back; "You won't stay up long?"

Peele grinned and settled herself into the chair with the first volume on her lap, "You know how a good read puts me to sleep..."

She opened the book.

My Dear Apprentice—

Primer of Basic Techniques:

Herein you will find A to Z everything you need to get started—refer back when necessary. For the sake of simplicity, all clay referred to in the subsequent chapters is Sculpey Premo! by Polyform.

Antiquing: Antiquing is the process of adding 'age' to a piece of work, generally by adding a thin layer of acrylic paint to the cured surface and then quickly wiping it off, leaving paint in the crevices and cracks. This technique is an art, not a science; there is no one way to do it. Experiment with different viscosities and colors, use multiple washes of different colors, try lighter colors over darker and vice versa. If you look at any ordinary rock in your yard closely, you will likely be amazed at how many different colors are present in a 'white' rock. Try different removal methods until you find the one that works best for you; fingers, baby wipes, and cosmetic sponges are all good choices. Acrylic paint is not your only option—oil paint, chalks, wood stains, dry tempera paint, even ashes from your fireplace can be used for authentic aging.

Basic Tool Kit for Polymer Clay:

The essential tools for working with polymer clay include:

Work surface of ceramic or marble tile

Pasta Machine, motor if desired

Oven for curing with free standing thermometer

Cardboard or tile curing surface for oven, PolyFil or cotton to cushion rounded forms and/or

Aluminum baking box with lid to protect against spiking temperatures; fill with baking soda or cornstach.

Timer

Cutting blades, stiff and flexible

Craft knife

Piercing needles, fine and thick

Cardstock or index cards

Hand roller or brayer

Quilting grid, ruler, graph paper for measuring

Jeweler's pliers; cutters, round nose and flat jaw

Liquid polymer clay for bonding cured and

raw clay: Translucent Liquid Sculpey, Fimo Deco Gel, Kato Clear Medium, Kato Polypaste, or Sculpey Bake 'n' Bond

Wet dry sandpaper in grits from 320 to 2000 for sanding, soft cloth for buffing to a high shine

Glazes: Future Acrylic Floor Polish, Sculpey Glaze, Varathane, or museum grade paste wax (Renaissance Wax)

Scissors

Stylus, knitting needles or other clay shaping tools

Release agents: water mister, cornstarch, or Armor All

Glues for attaching findings: E-6000, Mod Podge, Two part epoxy, or Cyanoacrylate/Zap a Gap

Clay: Polymer clay is first and foremost a plastic compound. It is in fact simply another form of PVC—the strong inert plastic that pipes are constructed from. The cognomen 'clay' refers to its malleability. The clay used by the authors is Sculpey Premo!; easily obtainable, it is our preferred medium for its ease of use, superior strength, and color palette, which closely follows that of painters, and so removes much guesswork from color mixing. Other artist grade clays include Kato Polyclay, Fimo Classic and Soft, Pardo, and Cernit. Each have their virtues, and are well worth exploring. Curing temperatures vary between brands; the author's experience is that they may be mixed without hesitation, so long as one cures to the temperature of the highest curing clay in the mix.

Conditioning: All polymer clay must be made soft and pliable before using. Slice clay very thin (1/8") and run through a pasta machine on the second thickest setting, joining slices after each pass until you have one large sheet; fold this sheet and run through the pasta machine on the same setting, turning the folded sheet one-quarter turn before each pass through the machine. The clay is fully conditioned when it shows no cracks at the fold. As a general rule, it takes the same number of passes through the machine to fully condition as it does to completely blend two colors. Should your clay crumble, the following remedies can be applied: place the clay in a sturdy plastic bag, and hammer with a rubber mallet until it forms a sheet; or, process it for a few pulses in a dedicated food processor; or add Mineral Oil or Clay softener; or add up to 1/3 its volume in a soft translucent clay.

Curing: All polymer clay must be thoroughly cured for strength. The manufacturer's recommendations are on the package, but as a general rule cure to 275 degrees F for at least 20 minutes per each quarter inch of thickness. Some clays cure at different temperatures so always check for the brand you are using. If mixing brands, cure to the temperature of the highest curing brand. To protect against scorching, cover the object with foil or encase it in a lidded 'baking box' which you can construct with foil or other metal pans. Filled with cornstarch or baking soda, it will further protect against scorching. Light colored pearlescent clays are especially vulnerable to scorching; monitor these carefully. The top element of the oven is usually the culprit, so observe your oven for 'spikes' and always use an oven thermometer. The 'longer the stronger', so if the piece you are creating has delicate appendages, you may wish to use several shorter cures. Many complex pieces require several curings; always use liquid clay to adhere cured and raw clay. Translucent clays deepen in color—cure a small sample to see the final color before committing large amounts of clay.

Drilling: Drilling cured clay results in a more professional look in most cases. It pays to obtain a good quality variable speed drill that can take a variety of small bits. Many artists find it easier to get consistent results by immobilizing the drill and bringing the object to it. It is helpful to mark the object with a 'pilot' hole, and when the bit has penetrated the object, turn it frequently and observe if the path is straight from all angles. If you should emerge in an unwanted area, patch the error with clay, re-cure for 10 minutes, and drill again. It is also helpful to drill halfway through, withdraw and drill from the opposite side until the two channels meet. For large objects, a piece of thin tape adhered to the surface will provide a visual guide. For drilling parallel channels, use a corn cob holder to mark the paths of the drill. Always match the size of the drill bit to the desired stringing material—in most cases, the bit should be slightly larger than the stringing material. *As an alternative to drilling, see Piercing.*

Embedding: To secure wires in raw clay, form a tiny 'hook' with pliers on the end of the wire which will be pushed in the clay; when pushed in the clay to the desired depth, press gently to secure it around the wire. After curing, you may insure the bond with a small drop or cyanoacrylate glue. When embedding smooth objects, push a small amount of raw clay over the sides of the object to hold it.

Extruding: Using a device which creates specific shapes, such as v-shaped ribbons, in polymer. Raw well-conditioned polymer is packed into the barrel, a die of the desired shape is secured to the end, and the polymer is forced out through the die. Color blend effects may be produced by stacking different colors of polymer into the barrel in sequence. Most extruders operate by manual pressure, either by a screw mechanism or compression. It pays to obtain a quality extruder.

Glazing: Though there is nothing quite as wonderful as a flawless polish, occasionally glazes are required to protect a surface finish, such as mica powders, metal pulvers or chalk, or to impart a high gloss. Information on nearly all of them can be found on the web—as a rule of thumb, if it cleans up with water, it's safe for polymer. Solvent based glazes can be problematic and should be avoided. Preferred glazes are: Future Floor Polish, Kato Clear Medium, Rustoleum Varathane, Two part resin, and Renaissance Wax. Note that Kato Clear Medium requires high curing with both an oven and a heat gun for maximum clarity; and Renaissance Wax can only be obtained in most cases through an internet supplier. Both are superior products with many applications. Future

Floor polish, widely available, can be diluted to produce a less glossy finish that is still durable. Two part resin, while a bit messy to work with, is the gold standard for a hard glossy finish.

Leaching: Clay that is too soft (fresh) may be made stiffer by placing the sheet of clay between two pieces of ordinary copy paper overnight; the oily residue on the paper is your indication that the clay is leached and ready for use. (Very helpful in caning, as soft clay will distort)

Measurements: The clay used throughout this book, Premo!, is sold in 2 oz. blocks which are scored into quarters. (Larger bricks are available as well, but almost exclusively online.) Where fractions are specified as measurements, they refer to the fraction of the whole block—i.e., to obtain 1/8 of a block, one cuts the whole block into 4 equal pieces along the score lines, and then cuts one of the four pieces in half. One half of one fourth = one eighth. One half of one eighth = one sixteenth. Except where noted, in formulas where 'dots' are referred to, they will be 3/4" circles of clay cut from sheets rolled to the thickest setting of the pasta machine.

Mica clays: Also known as metallic or 'pearl' clays, they contain microscopic grains of mica to make them appear 'shimmery' or pearlescent. The most common colors are gold, silver, copper and pearl, though now many manufacturers offer a wide variety of colors. They all share common characteristics. Once conditioned, they can be 'burnished' by rolling the sheet several times more through the pasta machine, either reducing the thickness each time, or folding and rolling on the same thickness; the key is to always send the clay through in a same direction (vertical). An observable change in brightness results. This is critical in the technique known as 'mica-shift' or 'ghost shift' where a burnished sheet of metallic clay is heavily impressed with a design, then the surface is minutely shaved with a very sharp blade to reveal the 'end grain' or dull areas of the clay. The result is a strikingly 3-dimesional holographic image on flat clay.

Piercing: Raw (uncured) clay is pierced for stringing by using a two-step approach. First, let the clay rest and cool after it is formed. Then pierce through with a very thin needle to create a pilot hole; follow that path with a needle the size of your stringing material. When going through the clay, twirl your needles constantly.

Polishing: Many techniques call for polishing the surface of the clay, as it naturally cures to a matte finish. (Kato is the exception to this). To polish, begin by sanding with wet-dry medium, and progress through the grits to the finest one which accomplishes the desired surface. Suggested range is 400-2000. Following sanding, the work can be buffed on a machine (take care against flinging and burning), with coarse cloth such as denim, or on ordinary cut-pile carpet. A polish may also be achieved with a surface finish; see Glazing above.

Reducing: In canes, to decrease the overall diameter of the cane by stretching, pinching, pressing or rolling. As it lengthens, this creates ever smaller patterns in the cane, and increases the number of slices which can be obtained. In sheets, to reduce the distance of the rollers from each other in order to lengthen the sheet and make it thinner; after each pass through the machine, turn the dial one notch so the rollers mover closer together and roll the clay through; it is very important to not skip a step. Also called stepping down.

Sheeting: Rolling clay through the pasta machine to form a sheet. Start with the 2nd-thickest setting. (Look down at the machine as your turn the dial to determine if the rollers are moving farther apart or closer together). To reduce your sheet (make it thinner and longer), turn the dial to the next thinnest setting on each pass to create thinner sheets. Also called stepping down. Never skip a step.

See the chart below for determining the setting of your pasta machine, as numbers vary from brand to brand:

Thickest setting:	**9 standard playing cards fit between the rollers**
Medium thick setting:	**4 standard playing cards fit between the rollers**
Medium:	**3 standard playing cards fit between the rollers**
Medium Thin:	**2 standard playing cards fit between the roller**
Thinnest setting:	**1 standard playing card fits between the rollers**

Skinner Blend: A technique originated by Judith Skinner, this method creates a seamless color blend of two or more colors in a single sheet of clay. The basic method (there are many variations) consists of joining two sheets of clay cut into right triangles along the longest edge. The resulting sheet is folded bottom to top and rolled through the pasta machine at the same thickness of the original sheets. As the sheet emerges from the roller, fold bottom to top and send through again. (It is critical to fold the sheet the same way and send it through the machine fold first each time.) After several passes through the machine, the colors will begin to blend across the width of the sheet; continue until you are satisfied with the result. (Also known as a Gradient Blend) To lengthen a blend, after the final pass, fold the sheet as usual, turn it one-quarter turn so that the fold is vertical, and send through the machine on the same setting; then step the machine down and thin the sheet until it reaches the desired thickness. *(See Reducing)*

Snakes and logs: Cylinders of clay formed by rolling strips of clay on a smooth surface. Snakes are generally smaller than logs. Tiny snakes can also be referred to as strings. Use the flat of the hand and gentle pressure; if ridges or bumps are visible, use less pressure. Very smooth snakes may be obtained by rolling the clay with cardstock or an acrylic block.

Surface Techniques: Altering the appearance of the polymer by treating the surface with any number of agents; mica powders, metal pulvers, chalks, paints, dyes, metal leaf and iridescent foils are but a few. Often used in imitative techniques to suggest other materials such as metal.

Texturing: Using tools and material to create a surface design on the clay; very useful for hiding imperfections and joins. Ordinary household items like sandpaper, sponges, etc. can create very interesting effects—always experiment. Un-mounted rubber or silicone stamps are also very useful.

A Scandal in Bronze, Silver, & Gold

Celtic Bronze Fibula

My Dear Apprentice—

The alchemists of old sought in vain to turn lead into gold—silly creatures; one must achieve only the appearance, not the fact. Dear, lamented Pinchbeck knew this perfectly well and profited by it. As shall we.

Tools:

Oven for curing

Pasta machine

Curing surface (cardboard)

Work surface (ceramic tile)

Hand roller or brayer

Piercing tools—needles, rods, stir straws, etc.

Texturing tools such as metal tubing, ball styli, etc.

Spray bottle for water

Index cards or deli paper

Texture sheets—your choice

Soft brushes for dusting mica powders

Firm brush for applying antiquing (paint)

Q-tips

Supplies:

1 blocks worth of dark scrap clay, including some metallic colors.

OR : 1/4 block each of Premo! Black, Gold, Silver, Blue Pearl.

OR: 1/2 block each of Green pearl and Copper.

OR: 1 block of Bronze.

Pearl-ex in various colors—Bronze, Copper, Gold, Magenta, Deep Blue, Deep Purple, Green, etc.

Black acrylic paint

Curved curing surface

Future clear floor polish or other light-body glaze

Metal, glass, or other inclusions (if desired)

Turkey lacing pin (either with eye or bent end), or wooden skewer

Celtic Bronze Fibula

Step 1: Create bronze

There are several ways to do this; the first and simplest is to use the scrap on hand, and tweak the color to suit your whim. Roll all of your dark scrap together; then add Gold or other metallic clays until the color pleases you.

Keep your basic color training in mind; if your mix is too cool, add warm colors—if too warm, add cool colors.

The second approach is more methodical. Combine equal amounts of Black, Gold, Blue Pearl and Copper.

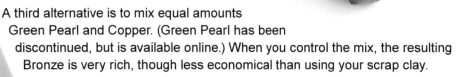

A third alternative is to mix equal amounts Green Pearl and Copper. (Green Pearl has been discontinued, but is available online.) When you control the mix, the resulting Bronze is very rich, though less economical than using your scrap clay.

If you can, it is best to mix up several different shades of Bronze, each a bit different; when you combine them on larger pieces, the differences are subtle but effective.

You can do this by mixing up one batch of Bronze and dividing it in three—leave one, and add different colors of clay to the others; they will harmonize because they are from the same base—sharing the same mother, as it were. (As a last resort, there is now a Premo! Bronze.)

Take a look at the different color combinations; the first is just scrap clay with enough Gold added to give it depth; the others are precisely mixed samples.

left to right:
Scrap Bronze, Blue Pearl/Black/Copper/Gold Bronze,
and Copper/Green Pearl Bronze

25

Step 2: Celtic Fibula base

Take a piece of clay about the size of a walnut and roll it into a snake about 8" long, tapering both ends.

Use your fingers to form it into a figure 8 shape, making sure the ends meet and overlap in the center (for strength).

Check your pin to make sure the ends will rest securely on the base piece, reserving about 1/2" of the pin for the decorative cap, and keeping in mind that the entire brooch will be bent into a curve, shortening the distance the pin must span.

Working on an index card, pull the overlapping ends off so that you can work with a flat surface.

Decide what texture you wish for the back of your piece, mist it with water, and flatten the base with your fingers or an index card onto a texture of some sort—stair tread and coarse sandpaper are good for this.

Work from the center out. A 'fat' middle is desirable from a design standpoint.

Choose a texture sheet, mist with water and impress a texture into the top of the base.

Once you have textured the entire piece, replace the overlapping ends to their original position.

Press them down gently to insure adhesion.

Take your remaining bronze clay(s) and sheet through your pasta machine, stepping down the thickness to medium. (3 playing cards—See Primer-Reducing.)

Texture these sheets and cut into various sized strips, then cut some of those strips into triangles, rectangles and squares.

Use your needle tool, blade ends or ball styli to further texture these small pieces as you press them firmly onto the base piece. Their placement should not interfere with the path of the pin—check to make sure.

Step 3: Spirals and beads

Roll tiny bits of your scrap into strings, about 1-2" long, then taper these strings on each end.

Using your fingers, gently roll these strings into tiny flat spirals—either single or double.

Place these on your base and gently press with an index card or deli paper to adhere to the raw clay beneath. If you wish to add metal or glass embellishments, now is the time.

For beads, roll random sized balls between your fingers and place where you wish—clusters look best for the smaller ones, and the larger ones can be flattened and textured.

Beads are extremely useful for hiding mistakes!

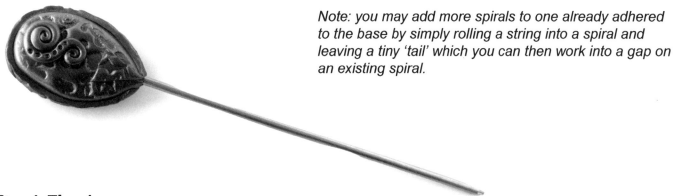

Note: you may add more spirals to one already adhered to the base by simply rolling a string into a spiral and leaving a tiny 'tail' which you can then work into a gap on an existing spiral.

Step 4: The pin

If using the turkey lacer needle, encase the bent end or 'eye' completely in clay and shape as you desire, texturing and decorating it as you did the brooch itself. You may wish to create a design that will complement the brooch where it will rest, or use a separate design element.

The pin may turn and designs on both sides are a good idea. Metal is preferred, but you may use a sanded wooden skewer or any material that can withstand 275 degrees F. If skilled in metalwork, you can forge a custom pin from thick bronze or copper wire, which gives you a wonderful authentic look. If using wood, seal it to prevent splinters.

Step 5: Coloring your brooch and pin.

Coloring clay to give it the appearance of metal is an exercise in restraint. Pretend you are applying eye shadow. While Bronze appears to be a uniform color, the reality is that it consists of several different colors; never use less than four.

Begin by lightly dusting on the bronze color. If you brush and re-brush areas without adding more powder, it will burnish the surface and deepen the color. Tap your brush against the rim of the jar when you refill it.

Leave some areas bare—you can always come back and place another color there. Let the beauty of the Bronze you created show through.

After you have applied a light coat of the Bronze, apply the other colors one at a time to tint different areas of your design. Overlap without hesitation. Be sparing with powerful colors like purple and blue. When applying coloring agents to your clay go all the way down the sides, and turn your work frequently to view it from all angles

Once you are satisfied with both fibula and pin, shape your brooch by gently curving the index card so that the ends are lower than the center—this will make it easier to insert the pin.

Once you are happy with the shape, remove your brooch from the index card and place the brooch on a rounded object like a slightly flattened paper tube covered with aluminum foil or something similar to maintain the curve.

Small pieces of rounded ceramic wall tile are great curing surfaces for curved polymer—look in the tile section of home improvement stores.

"This is really wonderful, Noelia." said Peele,

"Look how the colors all blend so smoothly—it really does look like bronze."

Step 6: Curing and sealing

Preheat your oven using a thermometer to the temperature recommended on the package. (See Primer—Curing). Place your work (and form) on the cardboard and put it in the oven until fully cured. If you have used scrap, you may have an unpredictable mix of clay, and the recommendation is to cure slightly longer than usual—dark clay will not burn if the oven temperature stays steady, though you may wish to cover it lightly with a piece of foil to shield the top..

Once the pieces are fully cured, (40 minutes is the recommended minimum time) remove from the oven and let cool on the form. When

fully cooled, lightly glaze all the colored surfaces, (See Primer, Glazing) and let dry. You may wish to rest it on top of your oven or other warm place to help set the glaze.

Step 7: Antiquing.

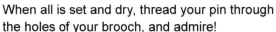

When your glaze is completely dry, apply black acrylic paint with a stiff bristled brush—old toothbrushes work well. Dab a bit of paint on the brush and work it down into the design, getting the paint into all the crevices and patterns that you can in one small area. (See Primer—Antiquing).

Using a clean damp finger, baby wipe, or sponge, quickly wipe the black paint off the high areas, leaving the paint in the recesses for an 'aged' look.

Do small areas at a time, and work quickly as acrylic paint dries fast.

Applying a diluted coat of glaze after it has thoroughly dried will make the colors more striking, however this is a matter of preference. Glazes dry even more quickly than paint, so rinse your brush immediately after use.

When all is set and dry, thread your pin through the holes of your brooch, and admire!

Parker frowned as she looked over the drawing, "This is such a strange style of jewelry, Peele."
Miss Peele looked over her companion's shoulder. "Oh, that," she said, "came out of the Pueblos up North, back in the 80's—some Navajo fellow. Very bold, but I can't see it ever catching on." She paused, "I say," she said thoughtfully, "it is a bit unusual to have such an obscure style in the collection. I wonder..."

Navajo Silver Pendant

These same basic techniques can be used to create bezels and settings for heat-resistant gemstones or polymer clay cabochons. Mica powder comes in silver, gold and copper colors, but to imitate these metals there are true metal powders (pulvers) available that do the job better.

Metal powders are much more opaque than mica, and 'harden' under the heat necessary to cure the polymer, creating a surface more resistant to scuffing. Because they contain pulverized metal, observe the precautions called for by the manufacturer.

For silver and gold, use mica clays of the same color as the metals you are imitating.

Tools:

Oven for curing

Pasta machine

Curing surface (cardboard)

Work surface (ceramic tile)

Hand roller or brayer

Piercing tools—needles, rods, stir straws, etc.

Texturing tools such as metal tubing, ball styli, etc.

Craft knife

Q-tips

Spray bottle for water

Index cards or deli paper

Texture sheets—your choice

Soft brushes for dusting mica powders

Firm brush for applying antiquing (paint)

Supplies:

1 block Premo! Silver

1/4 Block Premo! Pearl

1/8 Block Premo! White

Turquoise cab or bead

Coral nugget beads

Silver metal powder (Mona Lisa recommended)

Black acrylic paint

Glaze

Step 1: Mix the silver clay

Condition and mix together all clays until the color is uniform. Roll the clay into a thick log. Cut off a small section of the log—about 1/4" in thickness, and roll into a ball. Flatten the ball slightly on an index card, making sure that it is deep enough to contain your coral or turquoise.

Step 2: Create the settings for the stones

Press the turquoise firmly into the clay until the sides are covered. Using your fingers, press the clay toward the sides of the turquoise at the slight angle, sloping down from the top of the stone. (If using a bead, make sure to cover the holes). Use your blade to cut the clay away from the stone, a rough shape at first, then 'nibble' away at the edges and corners until the shape conforms to that of the stone. (If you accidentally cut into the side of the stone, patch and re-cut.) Gently smooth the clay around the stone to soften the edges. Use a needle or other tool to indent tiny lines in the upper edges of the clay where it meets the stone to create the illusion of a gallery bezel

Repeat this process with the coral nugget beads, choosing the best side to present and covering the holes as well as you are able. Though different levels will add interest, try to keep the stones and settings at a relatively uniform depth.

Step 3: Create the pendant base

Sheet your remaining silver clay on a medium setting—about 3 playing cards.

Use a damp (misted) texture sheet to embellish the surface.

Place this base on an index card and place your stones in their settings on the base—try different designs until you are satisfied, leaving room for any clay elements you will create.

Once you have determined the final placement, press down gently.

Use an craft knife to cut out the shape of the pendant, leaving enough room to introduce other elements.

Gently smooth the edges of your pendant with a modeling tool or fingers, pressing along the base of each element to secure them.

Continuing to work on an index card, dust your clay all over lightly with the silver powder, brushing and re-brushing areas to achieve good coverage. Use small amounts; the mere act of brushing will deposit more metal on the surface, and burnish it to a shine.

Cure at the recommended temperature (See Primer, Curing) for 15 minutes.

Let cool, then flip your textured sheet face down and applying a small amount of liquid clay to your cooled pendant, place it on the raw clay and trim the edges to fit.

Apply liquid clay all around the edge of the pedant base. Roll a thin snake of Silver clay and twist it into a rope; apply it carefully all around the pendant base, trim the ends flush, and smooth the seam.

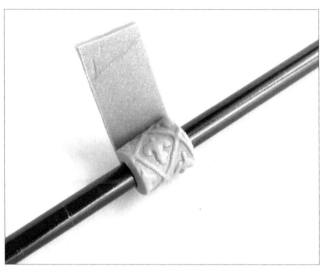

Step 4: Adding a bail and embellishments

Apply a small amount of liquid clay to the area where you wish to place the bail.

Roll a small strip of the textured clay around a tool the size of the hole you wish, cut it flush, and press both clay and tool against the top of the pendant; twist the tool gently to remove.

Create elements to add to your design; roll thin snakes and balls of clay, and form some of the balls into teardrops. Flatten these slightly.

Use a thin needle tool to press lines into the teardrops to form leaves or feathers. (one line down the center, several diagonal lines angling away from the center line). Leave some balls plain.

"Our nemesis makes this sound so easy;" grumbled Parker, "shapes as complex as leaves formed with just straight lines?"

Peele handed her the index card "See for yourself—these took less than a minute."

Parker whistled softly. "Well, I'll be cornnobbled!"

Apply these as you wish on your pendant, using liquid clay to insure good adhesion and arranging the elements to disguise any flaws or joins.

Dust your pendant with the silver powder, taking care to cover every area. The back is optional but recommended.

"Confound it!" cried Parker; "I've got silver dust all over my stones."

Peele handed her an object without looking up. "A damp Q-tip works wonders. Carry on."

Cure for 30 minutes. Cool completely and check all joins for strength—if any seem insecure, apply liquid clay to the areas and re-cure for 20 minutes.

Step 5: Finishing

Apply a light coat of glaze to the entire pendant and after it dries, apply a wash of black paint to antique it. (See Primer, Antiquing). When you are pleased with the effect, let dry and apply one final coat of glaze to areas you wish to highlight. This is optional but enhances the look of the metal. String your creation as desired. Good choices are turquoise and coral nugget beads, and silver.

Art Nouveau Gingko Brooch

"This is that style that's all the rage in Paris this year," observed Peele. "All twining plants and women with unkempt hair swooning on divans."

"Oh I don't know," ventured Parker; "it's rather dreamlike. Besides, I love dragonflies."

"Hmph" sniffed Peele. "I'm glad my hair knows its place; and I'm certainly not wearing insects, however artistically made."

Tools:

Oven for curing

Pasta machine

Curing surface (cardboard)

Work surface (ceramic tile)

Hand roller or brayer

Piercing tools—needles, rods, stir straws, etc.

Texturing tools such as metal tubing, ball styli, etc.

Craft knife

1" circle cutter

1.5" oval cutter

Spray bottle for water

Index cards or deli paper

Texture sheets—your choice

Soft brushes for dusting mica powders

Firm brush for applying antiquing (paint)

Supplies:

1 Block Premo! Gold (either standard or 18k--your choice)

1/2 block of Premo! Black

Lisa Pavelka transfer foils OR Jones Tones transfer foils (your choice)

Teardrop shaped embellishment (your choice), such as a pearl, glass bead, or gemstone--anything but real opal.

Heavy body acrylic metallic paint—(Liquitex iridescent rich copper recommended)

Gold metal powder (Mona Lisa recommended)

Glaze (Future recommended)

Standard brooch back

Art Nouveau Ginko Brooch

Step 1: Creating the leaves

Thoroughly condition your Gold clay (See Primer, conditioning) then roll and fold it several times more, sending it through the pasta machine always in the same direction to 'burnish' the surface and create maximum shine (See Primer, Mica Clays).

Thin this sheet by stepping the pasta machine down one step at a time until you reach a medium thickness (See Primer, reducing), about 3 playing cards.

Work on an index card, and cut 3 1" circles from your sheet.

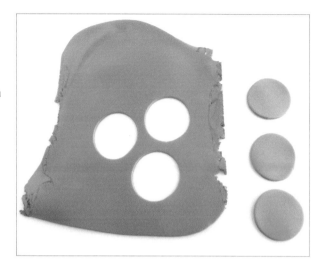

Lightly mark a line down the center of each circle, and using the circle cutter, cut two almond shapes from each side, leaving a thin 'tail' down the center line.

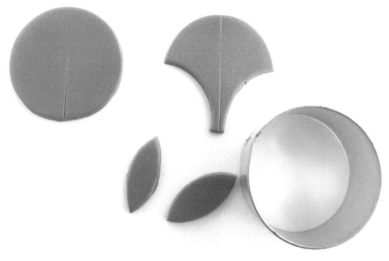

Use your blade to cut a 'notch' from the rounded edge of each leaf—at least one.

Thin the forward edges of the leaves with your fingers, ruffling and distorting as you go.

Roll a thin snake of Gold clay about 2" long and roughly the thickness of the 'tail' of each leaf. While flattening the end of the snake, attach it to the bottom of the leaf, smoothing the join lightly.

Taper the other end of the snake to a point.

Use your needle tool to draw thin fine lines on the leaves, following the curve of the leaf, overlapping the lines and using both short and long strokes.

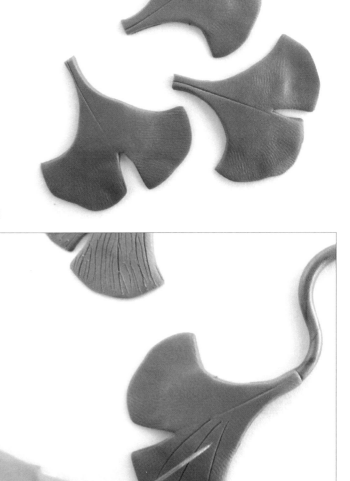

"Hmmm," murmured Peele, "now I see why we're using these cards to work on—makes everything so much easier turning the work and drawing from different angles."

40

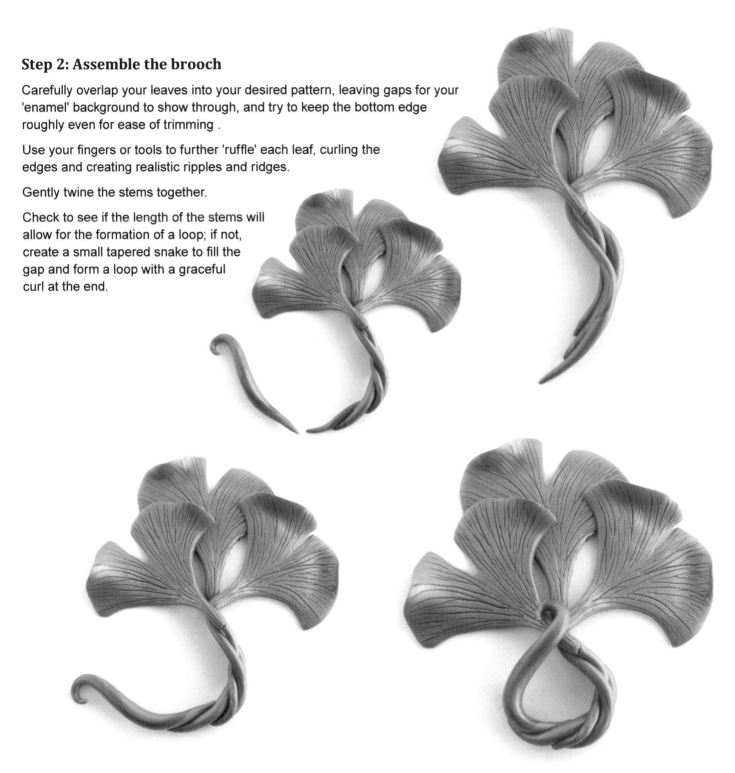

Step 2: Assemble the brooch

Carefully overlap your leaves into your desired pattern, leaving gaps for your 'enamel' background to show through, and try to keep the bottom edge roughly even for ease of trimming .

Use your fingers or tools to further 'ruffle' each leaf, curling the edges and creating realistic ripples and ridges.

Gently twine the stems together.

Check to see if the length of the stems will allow for the formation of a loop; if not, create a small tapered snake to fill the gap and form a loop with a graceful curl at the end.

Thoroughly brush the top of your creation with the gold powder, brushing and re-brushing areas to insure complete coverage.

Be sure to address the areas of the leaves which have curled up, and pay special attention to the loop. (In a subsequent step a piece of raw clay will pass through, and good coverage insures that it will not bond to the loop).

Cure at the recommended temperature for 20 minutes and cool thoroughly. (See Primer—curing).

Seal with a light coat of glaze to protect the surface.

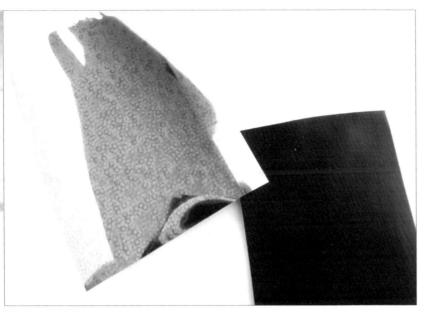

Step 3: Create the faux enamel background

Select the transfer foil you desire. Roll a sheet of Black clay to a medium thin thickness roughly the size of the leaf area, and burnish the foil sheet **pattern side up** onto the lack clay. (See the instructions with the foil for complete details).

When adhesion is complete, tear away the foil sheet in one swift motion. If there are large gaps you may replace the sheet and re-burnish.

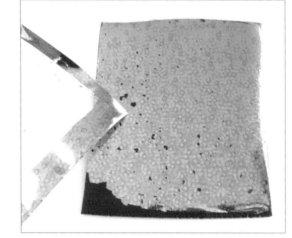

Use your 1.5" oval cutter to cut out a section of the 'enameled' sheet, and after applying liquid clay to the back of the brooch, position the brooch onto the enameled oval so that the bright areas show through the gaps in the leaves; turn the brooch over and gently press the black clay against the brooch, smoothing the edges down.

Turn the brooch face up and use an craft knife to trim the bottom and any other edges away. Smooth any rough edges and cure at the recommended temperature for 10 minutes.

Step 4: Create the drop

Select the item which will form the drop; in this example,
a baroque glass bead. Working on an index card, roll a ball of gold
clay roughly twice the size of the bead and press the bead firmly into
it, pressing the sides of the clay up very snug against the surface and
angling the clay down from the top.

Cut away from the sides until you have
formed a thin bezel around the
bead, and smooth with your
fingers.

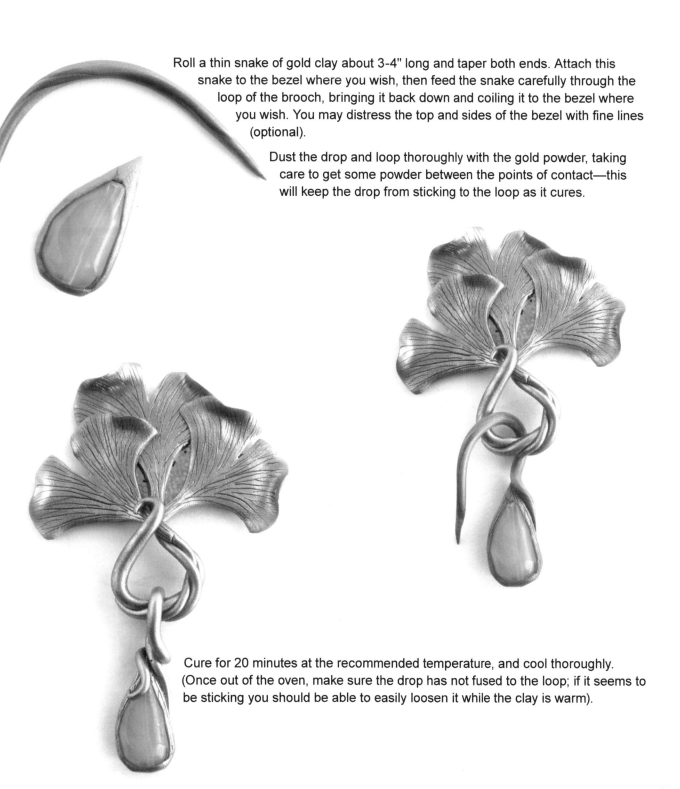

Roll a thin snake of gold clay about 3-4" long and taper both ends. Attach this snake to the bezel where you wish, then feed the snake carefully through the loop of the brooch, bringing it back down and coiling it to the bezel where you wish. You may distress the top and sides of the bezel with fine lines (optional).

Dust the drop and loop thoroughly with the gold powder, taking care to get some powder between the points of contact—this will keep the drop from sticking to the loop as it cures.

Cure for 20 minutes at the recommended temperature, and cool thoroughly. (Once out of the oven, make sure the drop has not fused to the loop; if it seems to be sticking you should be able to easily loosen it while the clay is warm).

Step 5: Attach the pin back and finish

Roll a thin sheet of gold clay, (about 2 playing cards) and cut a 1.5" oval from it; apply liquid clay to the back of the enameled sheet, and cover it with the gold clay, smoothing the edges to the back of the brooch and trimming away any excess clay.

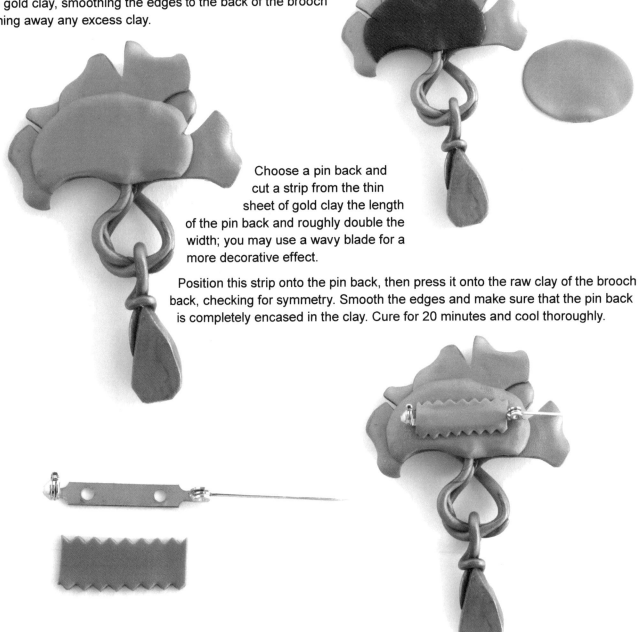

Choose a pin back and cut a strip from the thin sheet of gold clay the length of the pin back and roughly double the width; you may use a wavy blade for a more decorative effect.

Position this strip onto the pin back, then press it onto the raw clay of the brooch back, checking for symmetry. Smooth the edges and make sure that the pin back is completely encased in the clay. Cure for 20 minutes and cool thoroughly.

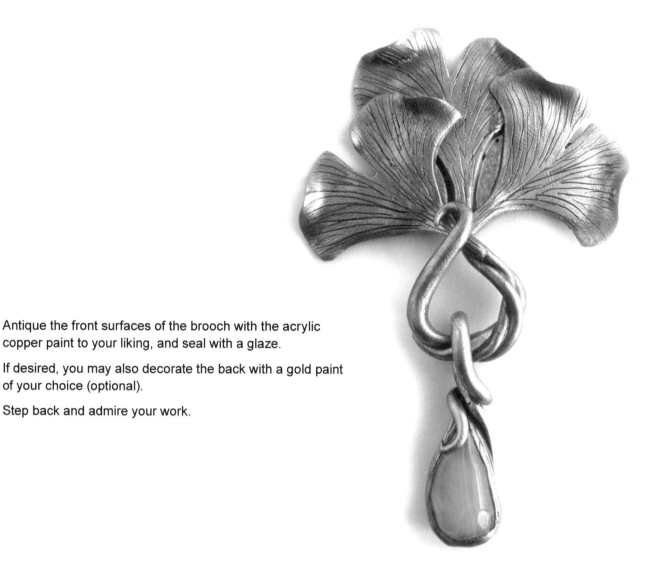

Antique the front surfaces of the brooch with the acrylic copper paint to your liking, and seal with a glaze.

If desired, you may also decorate the back with a gold paint of your choice (optional).

Step back and admire your work.

Congratulations My Dear Apprentice

You have completed the first and most important step in your career as a forger of jewels...use this knowledge to advantage in the years to come.

My Dear Apprentice

Carnelian, or Sard, as some would have it, is a gem of the greatest antiquity. It has been worked since the time of the Sumerian kings and Pharaohs of Egypt.

In ancient Rome it was the gem of choice for exquisitely carved seal rings. Inspired by a jewel that graced the throat of a Roman lady two thousand years ago, we shall now create a vibrant necklace.

Choker of Ancient Rome

A Study in Carnelian

Choker of Ancient Rome

Step 1 : Tint the clay and mix the colors

Condition and sheet out one package of the translucent clay to the thickest setting on your pasta machine.(9 playing cards. See Primer- conditioning, sheeting) Tint this sheet with 40 drops of Tangerine ink, 40 drops of Calabeza Orange ink and 10 drops of Burro Brown. Use your needle tool or a knitting needle mix the colors together and spread them out on the clay. Set aside for the ink to dry. This may take up to an hour if you are in a humid environment. This requires patience, but is much tidier than trying to mix in the ink while wet. Do NOT attempt to hurry the process with heat.

While the ink is drying, prepare the other block of translucent clay by thoroughly conditioning it and sheeting it to the thickest setting of your pasta machine.

When dry, mix the inks into the clay by folding and rolling it repeatedly through the pasta machine until well-colored but not completely uniform. A few subtle streaks are desirable.

From this point on, mixing the colors by hand gives a more natural appearance to the finished beads.

Cut a one inch strip from the tinted clay.

Place a drop or two of Burro Brown ink on a piece of plastic or other impervious surface.

With the needle tool apply the ink sparingly on the strip of clay. (you need not use it all) Let dry.

Fold the clay lengthwise with the ink in the center, fold in half the other way and roll between your palms. Fold again, twisting the roll a bit to distribute the ink.

Fold one last time and form into a snake, approximately 3/8 inch in diameter.

Set aside.

Supplies:

2 blocks of Premo! Translucent

Jacquard Pinata inks: Tangerine, Calabeza Orange, Burro Brown

Kosher salt

Off-white acrylic paint

Tools:

Basic tools for polymer clay (See Primer—basic tool kit)

Clay shaper with a tapered point

Knitting needle size 6 or 7

Electric Buffer

From your sheet of un-tinted clay cut as many approximately one inch strips as you can, and set aside.

From the tinted clay cut strips: 1/16 inch, 1/8 inch, ¼ inch, ½ inch and 1 inch wide.

Lay these tiny strips onto each of the un-tinted strips and roll and twist as before to blend the colors, stopping short of a uniform blend—streaks of color are desirable.

Roll each color into a 3/8" snake.

Mix any leftover scrap the same way and roll into a 3/8" diameter snake.

Step 2: Forming the beads

Gloves are recommended for this part of the procedure to prevent fingerprints.

From the various colors of clay cut at least 17 5/8 inch pieces of clay.

Pinch and crush each piece of clay between your fingers to further soften the colors.

Roll the clay into a ball, then form a drop shape by rolling one end only, keeping the top of the drop shape rounded. (the tip must be substantial enough to be pierced.)

Should it get too pointed, press it against your work surface. Use your needle tool to pierce a hole a scant quarter inch below the top of the pointed end.

Soften this hole by gently twirling the clay shaper in each side of the bead hole; this is more in keeping with the appearance of ancient drilling techniques.

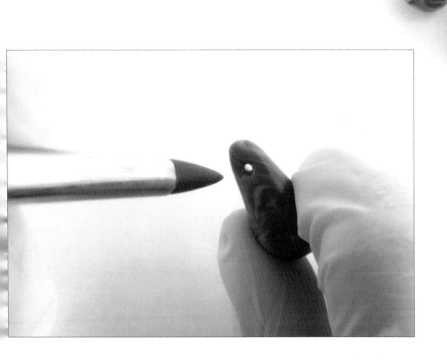

To replicate the pitting that forms on ancient beads which were buried underground, press a few pieces of Kosher salt onto some of the beads. Be sparing. Place about a teaspoon of salt onto a piece of paper and spread it thinly. Discard any leftover used salt afterwards.

As you finish each bead, place onto a sheet of batting, or into your pan of baking soda. (See Primer—curing)

Repeat for the other pieces of clay and be sure to vary the size and shape of your drops. Slight unevenness in size and shape is much more authentic.

When you have formed all of the drops, cut 36 to 38 3/8" pieces from the remaining snakes. Cut 10 to 12 more pieces, ¼" for smaller beads.

Roll all of them into round beads, but again, do not fret about perfection. Pierce each bead completely and soften the holes with the clay shaper as you did with the drops.

Cure at the recommended temperature for at least 40 minutes (See Primer—curing. Upon removing from the oven, plunge into a container of ice water for maximum clarity. Leave in the water until the salt dissolves. Drain and let dry.

"Oh my," laughed Peele," look at this! Centuries of decay achieved in moments, thanks to common salt— who would have thought?!"

Step 3: Finishing the beads and drops

In this case, a subtle shine is best—sanding is unnecessary. Press each of the round beads individually onto a knitting needle that fits snugly, and gently buff on an electric buffer by twirling the bead against the rotating surface. To polish the drops, slip a piece of craft wire through the hole and use the wire as a handle to buff the drop.

"Mercy!" cried Peele. "This buffing requires the lightest touch—merely kissing the surface."

"I know," winced Parker, retrieving a bead which had flown across the room. "Just a tad too much pressure and the bloody thing snatches it right out of my hand."

Antique the drops and beads with the off-white acrylic paint, using a coarse brush to apply the paint, pressing deep into the pits. Wipe off with a damp paper towel or clean finger. Re-polish, if necessary with a soft cloth (See Primer— antiquing).

Choker of Ancient Rome

Supplies:
Finished beads and drops
Stringing material (choice)
Clasp and jump rings
Crimps

Tools:
Crimping pliers

Step 1: Create the pattern

Sort the beads by size and color, and lay them out on a work surface with the largest in the center.

Cut a length of your chosen stringing material about 22-24".

Step 2: String the necklace

Beginning in the center of your pattern, string the largest of the drop beads. This is your 'lead' bead.

On either side of this, continue the pattern, alternating a drop and a round bead, mixing up the colors as you go until all the drop beads are used.

Continue stringing with round beads, finishing with the smallest ones. Check the drape and length of the necklace as you work until it reaches the desired length.

Add your clasp. After the final bead on one end, string on a crimp, then run your stringing material through a jump ring and back through the crimp and at least two of the beads to hide the end. Tighten the crimp.

Repeat for the other side, taking up the slack before crimping.

Open the jump rings and attach the clasp, closing the jump rings securely.

Put it on and admire what a lovely Roman matron you are!

"This really is a lovely color on me, don't you think Peele?"

Peele nodded sagely. "I should say red is indubitably your color, Parker," she replied.

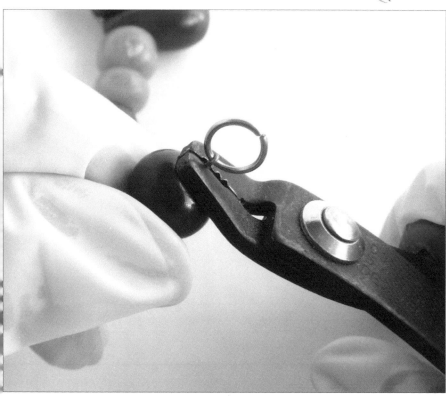

the Amethyst Ritual

Cabochons and Nugget Beads
Silver Art Nouveau Pendant

Supplies
Pinata Baja Blue Ink

Pinata Passion Purple Ink

Ranger Sunshine Yellow Ink

Jacquard Pearl-ex Macro Pearl Mica Powder

3 blocks Premo! White Translucent Clay

Tools
Standard Clay tools (See Primer—basic tool kit)

Cabochon mold (BestFlexibleMolds recommended)

Fine paintbrush

Batting (for curing rounded shapes)

Heat gun (for final cure out of the oven)

My Dear Apprentice

The ancient Greeks knew very well the properties of wine: how it freed both intellect and tongues; and they believed that the lovely purple gems which so resembled their favorite drink guarded them against the more extreme effects, by holding one in their mouths as they imbibed. It is certainly worth the experiment, is it not?

Step 1: Prepare the inclusions

On a piece of card stock chop 1/8 block of white translucent with about one quarter teaspoon of macro pearl mica powder. Pieces should be no larger than 1/8" in size.

Bake at the recommended temperature for ten minutes.(See Primer—curing)

While you may be tempted to bake these with your heat gun, don't try it unless you like to clean up mica powder.

After baking, take the card stock with the tiny pieces outdoors and gently blow off any extra mica powder.

> "Gently," said Peele, holding the card with the tiny bits of clay steady. "It is too easy to blow them all away..."

Step 2: The mother color

Sheet out the remaining clay from the first block. Add 4 drops of Passion Purple, 8 drops of Sunshine Yellow and 2 drops of Baja Blue inks. Spread out the ink with a needle tool or old knitting needle (the ink dries faster this way) and let dry. Blend into the clay with your pasta machine by folding and rolling on a medium setting (About 3 playing cards)

> Parker scratched her head; "Adding yellow seems strange, but as it's the color wheel compliment of violet, I see that it grays it down, and so seems more natural—wouldn't have thought of that in an age."

Step 3: Create a step blend

To prepare the clays we will do a step blend. As you blend up the original mother color, it will spread itself out to the width of the pasta machine.

Create a 'stepped' paper pattern: trim a piece of plain paper to about half the size of your clay sheet, fold it vertically into thirds, and from the middle column, cut down 1", and over to the edge, then cut down 1" on the last column and over to the edge. That will cover about half of the tinted (dark) clay.

Cut two shapes. Set aside the trimmings. Roll out two blocks of white translucent on the same thickness (medium) If your clay is very fresh it will tend to be sticky and harder to work with.

You can firm it up by sandwiching it between a couple of sheets of paper, cover with heavy books and set aside for an hour. This is called leaching. (See Primer—leaching)

Measure and lightly mark approximately 1/3 of the way down the sheet of white translucent, line up the center step with the mark and cut out.

You now have two sheets of white translucent, one larger than the other. Fit one shaped piece of mother color to each piece that you've cut from the white translucent clay, and join them by smoothing with your finger.

Don't worry about trimming the rounded edges on the bottom of each white translucent piece. Note that one sheet will be mostly Translucent, and one will be mostly purple.

58

Fold your sheets so that the translucent part rests on the colored part. Blend each sheet as you would for a Skinner blend. (See Primer— Skinner blend). You now have six different values of the amethyst colors.

Cut each color apart and lay out on your work surface.

Divide the lightest color in half.

To one part of this, dust with a layer of pearl mica powder, fold in half, and blend into the clay with your pasta machine.

Now for the fun part, My Dear Apprentice...

59

Step 4: Creating the beads

Tear small pieces from the different color sheets and press together to form a ¾ inch bead.

Smooth pieces by rolling between your palms until all the cracks are smoothed out. The colors will naturally bend and mix a bit to form the natural curves and layers.

Form ball into a nugget shape using your work surface and the heel of your hand. (Smooth fingerprints before curing to save sanding later).

To add inclusions, as you are adding your torn pieces, press several inclusion pieces, and any 'snakes' of pure color that you wish (from the trimmings) onto the clay and cover with a piece of the lightest color clay and roll smooth. You may also dig holes into the surface of your bead and drop tiny amounts of macropearl into the holes, then roll smooth.

If you plan to make the nugget necklace, make about 24 of these beads.

Roll between your hands until smooth. For beads, simply roll into your desired shape. Let cool before piercing if you do not plan to drill after curing. (See Primer—piercing)

Sand to at least 2000 grit and polish. (See Primer —polishing)

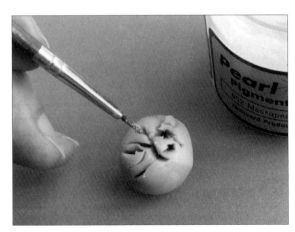

Step 5: Cabochons and finishing

You can also use the same technique to make cabochons. Stack and form a large enough ball to fill your desired mold.

Roll smooth, press into mold that has been coated with a release agent, (Cornstarch is perfect, but you may also spray your mold with plain water) trim excess clay with your blade and un-mold.

Cure at the recommended temperature (See Primer—Curing), and from the oven, blast briefly with a heat gun, then drop directly into ice water to increase the translucency. When cool, sand through progressively finer grits until at least 2000; polish to a high gloss, or use a glaze to bring up the shine.

String or set as desired.

"My goodness," said Parker, holding her new cabochon up to the light, "that trick with the heat gun and ice water really makes a difference; it's all in the details, isn't it?"

My Dear Apprentice

I trust you have kept in mind the directions for creating Faux Metal Settings for your work; here we will use the technique for silver—if you have forgotten, please refer back to that volume for the specifics.

Amethyst and Silver Art Nouveau Pendant

Supplies:

Cured and polished amethyst cabochon

½ block Premo! Silver clay

Mona Lisa Metal powder—platinum

Silver-colored eye pin

Donna Kato polypaste

White acrylic paint

Glaze (See Primer, Glazing)

Silver chain (optional)

Silver colored jump ring (optional)

Tools:

Standard clay tools—(See Primer, basic tool kit)

1" circle cutter

Flat soft-bristle paint brush

Fine tip soft-bristle paint brush

Step 1: Setting the base

Paint the back of the cabochon with white acrylic paint and set aside to dry. This prevents the silver backing from showing through the translucent stone and muddying the color. Take a 1½" eye pin, and bend a U-shaped 'hook' into the tail as shown. (This will be encased in the clay to form a firm anchor). Set it aside.

Condition and roll your silver clay to the thickest setting on the pasta machine (About 9 standard playing cards). Using your cutter, cut three 1" circles from the clay, and set two aside.

Take the third circle and stepping down the pasta machine one thickness at a time, (See Primer, sheeting) roll it through, giving the clay one-quarter turn after each pass to keep an oval shape, until you reach a medium thin thickness (about 2 playing cards)Texture the back if you wish. (optional) Lay the bent eye pin onto the front of the oval, keeping the loop clear, and pressing gently into the clay to form a level surface. Apply a thin layer of poly paste to the back of the cabochon and place it over the loop, centering it so that the loop is at the top and center of the cabochon. Press firmly and trim the clay around the cabochon, smoothing the edges and checking for good adhesion.

Step 2: Leaves and embellishments

Cut the other two circles in half. Discard one of the half circles, and nip off about a ¼ of one of the others .

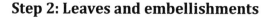

Roll one of the half-circles into a football shape; pinch and roll to form a 'tail' about 1 ½ " long—enough to curl into a spiral. Flatten the fat end of your shape into a leaf shape.

Thin the edges by pinching with your fingers and smooth any fingerprints. Use your needle tool to draw 'veins' in the leaf. The depth and placement is entirely up to you. (it is best to start with a center line and then draw the side lines).

Fold the leaf slightly and shape into a graceful drape. Repeat this process with other partial circles to end with two large leaves and one small one.

Step 3: Putting it all together

Apply a very small amount of poly paste to the backs of the leaves, and attach them to the surface of the cabochon with larger leaves at the bottom and smaller one up top—their placement is up to you. Drape the tails as you wish, forming at least one into a spiral for a design element.

Using your soft flat brush, liberally dust the metal powder onto your design, cleaning off any that gets onto the cabochon with a the fine-tipped brush dipped in alcohol, or a Q-tip.

Check for fingerprints or flaws, then cure at the recommended temperature for 30 minutes. When cool, apply the glaze of your choice (See Primer—glazing), attach a jump ring or bail to the loop, and string on chain as desired.

My Dear Apprentice

The great artist Kato outlined the basic method for creating Opal, that queen of gems, whose fire and flash have intrigued for centuries. In its many forms it is the stone of sight and prophecy, but also confers invisibility, and thus is the patronus of thieves.

The Greeks held it to be the tears of Zeus—god of the thunderbolt. Curiously, the Bedouins of Arabia say that it is formed when lightning strikes the desert sands. Whatever its origins, here we may easily make opals of surpassing beauty for mere pence...

Black Opal Cabochons
Barbarian Bracelet

the Adventure of the Spurious Opal

Black Opal Cabochons

Step 1: Create the opal matrix

In a small cup, mix together about a teaspoon each of the different colors of flakes.

Add a generous tablespoon of the Kato clear medium and mix lightly. The consistency should be that of sour cream.

Using a palette knife, spread this paste onto the surface of the tile or glass as thin as you possibly can; add more flakes to any areas which seem to be lacking and press them into the liquid with the knife.

Cure this amalgam on the tile at the recommended temperature for at least 20 minutes until it is clear; you may wish to give it a blast with the heat gun to achieve the maximum effect.

Supplies:

1/2 block Premo! Black clay

Large flake iridescent glitter (See secret sources) in at least two colors; suggested are Arnold Grummer Iridescent Flakes and Arnold Grummer Icy Blue Flakes

Kato clear medium

Iridescent dichroic film (See Secret sources)

Tools:

Basic tool kit (See Primer—basic tool kit for polymer clay)

Acrylic block

Ceramic or glass tile at least 4" square

Palette knife

Heat Gun

When cool, use your blade to gently peel up the sheet; note that the side in contact with the tile is quite smooth — this is the 'face' of your opal.

Turn your sheet face up and give it an additional blast with the heat gun to insure clarity, if necessary, and then turn the sheet face down again on the tile.

Cut a piece of the dichroic film roughly the size of your sheet, and using the heat gun, gently adhere the film to the sheet, moving the heat gun constantly, and keeping it well-centered to prevent 'flap-ups' of the film.

When the film has 'relaxed' into position, let cool, and flip the sheet over face up once more.

Trim to the edges even and observe the results.

Decide on the rough shapes of the gems you with to make, (keeping in mind that they will be encased completely in settings) and cut at least eight.

"Look at the fire of this," said Peele, "and see? It changes character completely depending on the background color."

"Yes," agreed Parker, "but I think it looks ever so lovely on the black."

Step 2: Form the base of the cabochons

Condition the black clay and roll it into various sized balls, (See Primer—Conditioning) flatten these with the acrylic block until they are about 1/8" in thickness.

Apply a very thin coat of Kato clear medium to the surface, and press one of your cut shapes deeply into the clay.

Use your blade to trim away the excess clay. Repeat this process for at least 7 more cabochons.

Cure the cabochons for 30 minutes at the recommended temperature. (See Primer—Curing).

Let cool, then apply a thin layer of Kato Clear medium to the surface. Cure again for 20 minutes and blast with a heat gun for maximum clarity.

Let cool, then repeat the process with at least one more coat (more if desired) until the surface is slightly domed and very clear. Set aside

"Mercy," declared Parker, waving the strange device in the air, "this heat pistol is a wonder—the surface looks like cloudy water and then suddenly becomes perfectly clear!"

"Aye," returned Peele "but have a care. I've scorched two already this morning —it just takes an instant. Keep it moving and don't get too close!"

Barbarian Bracelet

My Dear Apprentice

The origins of this unusual bracelet are quite shrouded in mystery. My father's oldest friend—a Romani cardsharp, magician and horse-healer—wore the original, and solemnly swore it came from lost Atlantis.

The style suggests the work of the Thracians, or Cimmerians, but who is to say? Its beauty is such, however, that I could not omit it from this collection.

Supplies:

1 block's worth of Bronze clay (See chapter on faux metals)

Stretch cord (Stretch Magic 1mm recommended)

Mica Powders (See chapter on Faux metals—Bronze)

7-8 cured opals

50 bronze or copper split rings, 6mm

Black acrylic paint

Glaze (Future recommended)

Cyanoacrylate glue (optional)

Alcohol (optional)

Tools:

Basic tools for polymer clay (See Primer —basic tool kit)

Texture sheet (choice) for bottom of settings

Ball Stylus, knitting needle, etc.

Corn cob holder

Other decorative texture (clear stamp recommended) for top of settings

Soft brushes

Coarse brush

Alcohol

Q-tips

Note: Measure your wrist to determine the number of links in your bracelet. 8" (or about 8 elements, depending on size) is standard, but if in doubt measure by wrapping a strip of paper around your wrist and add 5/8". Allow about 1/8" between each element for the spacers.

Barbarian Bracelet

Step 1: Create the bezels

Condition the bronze clay (See Primer — conditioning) and roll about one-third of the bronze clay into a strip about 10" long and 3" wide on a medium thin thickness. (2 playing cards)

Apply a small amount of liquid clay to the bottom of an opal, and place it on the bronze sheet. Trim around the base. Smooth the edges to insure good adhesion.

From the sheet, cut a strip roughly the height of the opal, and wrap it snugly around twice; on the second pass, slightly raise the strip over the inner layer. Cut where the ends overlap and smooth the seam.

Trim the edges flush with the bottom, and smooth the seams; check the top to see how much overlap there is on the surface of the opal, and trim if necessary, taking care to leave enough clay to thoroughly encase the opal and conceal the edges.

Smooth the top of the bezel, then use the texture to impress a light design. If the bezel distorts, smooth the inner line with a knitting needle or other tool.

Take a small portion of the sheet and impress it with the same decorative texture; cut this into thin strips for decorative elements.

Take other parts of the sheet and as with the Celtic Brooch (See Faux metals chapter, bronze fibula), create tiny decorative elements such as spirals, beads, crescents, etc. and place on the edges of the bezel.

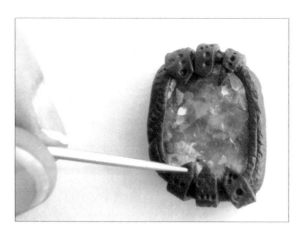

When placing these elements on the ends and sides of the setting, keep in mind that they should not interfere with the passage of stretch cord which will bind the bracelet.

Use your needle tool, knitting needle, ball stylus or blade to imprint further decorative designs such as dots or lines onto these elements, and the bezel itself both to add interest and to insure adhesion.

Repeat for the other opals.

When satisfied as to the design, dust your setting with at least four colors of mica powder, (See the chapter on faux metals —Celtic Brooch) and clean off any powder with clings to the surface of the opal with a soft brush or q-tip dipped in alcohol.

Cure at the recommended temperature for at least 30 minutes.

"Oh this is fun," said Parker, dotting away with her needle tool. "It's quite something that the repetition of just a few simple shapes can create such mysterious patterns—and these wee spirals are so cunning—like hieroglyphs."

"Closer than you know," replied Peele, "if this is truly an Atlantean design, legend has it that the Pharaohs were descended from those who fled the cataclysm."

Step 2: Finishing the elements

Roll a ball from the bronze clay and flatten, then roll it through the pasta machine on a medium setting (three playing cards). Texture this sheet, and placing it texture side down on an index card, apply a light coat of liquid clay to the bottom of an opal and press down firmly to the sheet. This extra layer will insure clean drilling.

Trim closely with a craft knife and smooth the seams, texturing the edges to hide the join.

Repeat for all of the opals.

Cure at the recommended temperature for at least 20 minutes. Let cool.

Lightly glaze all of the opals and let dry (See Primer—Glazing).

Apply black paint as an antique wash. (See Primer—Antiquing), wiping off the high areas until you are pleased with the effect. Let dry, and glaze again if desired. Let dry thoroughly.

Step 3: Drilling and stringing the elements

Decide on the layout of your bracelet, then mark each element with a corn cob holder.Drill two evenly spaced holes in each, remembering to go back through the opposite side to insure a clean hole.(See the chapter on Leopardskin Jasper page 102 for tips on drilling evenly).

Check the layout once more, and begin stringing. Between each element, string 3 or 4 of the 6mm split rings, according to your preference. Adjust the numbers if necessary to insure even spacing. Because the elements may have uneven sides, string both channels at the same time, pulling tight between each addition to insure an even hang and adjusting where necessary.

Tie off the ends in a triple overhand knot (See instructions for tying off bracelets in the Leopardskin Jasper chapter) and add a drop of cyanoacrylate glue for insurance.

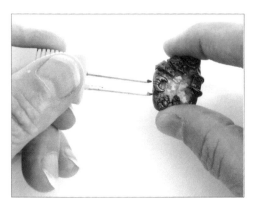  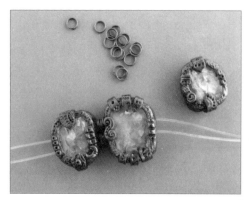

"Really marvelous," said Peele, holding up her wrist and turning it to admire the fiery flashes of her bracelet, "and our forger seems to have included it for mere sentiment—I do believe I see a chink in the armour."

A Question of Chrysoprase

Cabochons and Beads (A and B Grade)
Hammered Cuff Bracelet

My Dear Apprentice

Chrysoprase, that beautiful apple-green stone, is your next foray into the art of deception. Revered by the Greeks, King Alexander the Great wore this gem into battle and was never defeated. But one day he stopped to bathe in the Euphrates, casting aside his clothes and his precious talisman—and a serpent bore it off. He never won another battle, and died very young. It does not pay to be careless with objects of power. Happily, polymer reproduces this precious stone in all its marvelous variety.

Step 1: Tint the clay

Condition all of your white translucent (See Primer — conditioning) and sheet it to the thickest setting of your machine (See Primer—sheeting). Add to this sheet 4 drops of Lettuce ink, and 4 drops of Baja Blue. Spread over the surface, let dry, and blend into the sheet by folding and rolling it through the pasta machine until the color is uniform.

Decide at this point if you wish to create A or B grade chrysoprase: A grade is a uniform green color, whilst B grade has heavy black inclusions, or veining.

For A grade:

Add a very small amount of Pearl-ex Macropearl to the tinted clay by brushing it lightly onto the surface of the sheet with a soft-bristled brush. Use only as much as will adhere to the clay, and take it outdoors to blow off any excess. Blend this powder into the clay by folding and rolling it through the pasta machine several times. Let this sheet rest for a few moments.

For B grade:

Do NOT add any Pearl-ex to the sheet. Roll out the tinted sheet to the thickest setting of the pasta machine, fold double, and place in the freezer to chill while you prepare the cores.

Supplies:

1 block Premo! White Translucent clay

Ranger alcohol ink (Lettuce)

Pinata alcohol ink (Baja Blue)

½ block Premo! White

¼ block Premo! Ecru

Jaquard Pearl-ex Macropearl (optional)

Black acrylic paint

Tools:

Basic tool kit (See Primer— basic tool kit for polymer clay)

Soft-bristled flat brush

Cabochon Mold

Step 2: Form the beads and cabochons

For the bead core, mix 2 parts of white clay with 1 part of ecru. (The total amount depends on the number of beads or cabochons you wish to make).

For cabochons, roll out a ball of your core clay slightly smaller than is needed to fill the mold. For beads, roll out a ball that is approximately half the size of your final bead.

Take your tinted clay from the freezer and tear off small irregular pieces and place randomly on the core, leaving gaps between the pieces.

When satisfied with the coverage, use a small flat brush to work black acrylic paint into the gaps. (Do not trouble yourself about getting all the paint off the surface —you will be sanding down below this layer).

If you wish, wipe the excess paint from the surface, let dry for a few minutes, and roll between your hands until smooth.

Form this ball into either a bead or a cab.

For beads, simply roll into your desired shape.

Let cool before piercing if you do not plan to drill after curing.
(See Primer —piercing)

If making beads,cure at recommended temperature for at least 30 minutes. (See Primer—curing.)

Drop into ice water directly out of the oven to increase translucency. Sand and buff to a high gloss (See Primer—polishing).

"This is terribly messy," said Parker, staring in dismay at her blackened fingers.

"Dear Gel, Art is a messy process." replied Peele with some asperity.

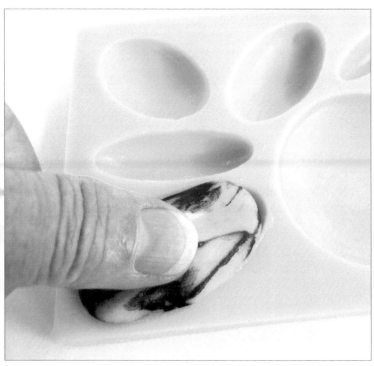

To use the cabochon mold, spritz lightly with water if it is not silicone (Silicone has a very rubbery feel) and after forming the ball into roughly the shape of the mold (to reduce waste), press firmly into the mold, shaving off the excess as shown, and unmold.

Alternatively, form your cabochon by hand.

Supplies:

Aluminum bracelet blank (shown is 1 1/2" wide)

1 block Premo! Gold or Silver clay (choice)

Metal powder (pulver) in gold , silver, or platinum (Mona Lisa Recommended)

Faux Chrysoprase cabochon (uncured, please see instructions below)

Liquid clay

Polypaste

Glaze (See Primer—glazing)

Tools:

Basic tool kit (See Primer—basic tool kit for polymer clay)

Clay shapers

Ball ended tool (Sculpey or other brand—your choice)

Soft bristled brushes 1/4" and 1/2" wide

Soft bristled detail brush

Cabochon mold (Example shown uses the 1.75" X .8" depression, but the size is up to you)

Examining gloves (optional but recommended)

Hammered Cuff Bracelet

Step 1: Form your cabochon

Form your cabochon as previously described, following the instructions to produce either A or B grade.

To make the cuff bracelet as shown, gently bend your raw cabochon to match the curve of the bracelet. Cure it on the cuff blank to insure a good fit, at the recommended temperature for at least 30 minutes. (See Primer—curing.)

Drop into ice water directly out of the oven to increase translucency. Sand and buff the cab to a high gloss (See Primer—polishing).

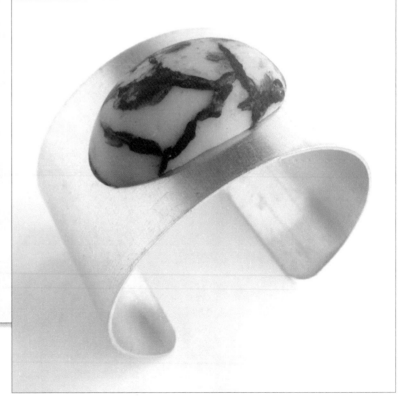

Step 2: Cover the cuff blank

Condition your preferred color of clay (Gold is shown as the example) and sheet to a medium thickness. (About 3 playing cards; See Primer—sheeting) Cut a strip the width of your blank and just slightly shorter than the total length. Sheet this strip to medium thin thickness (about 2 playing cards).

Adhere this strip to the inside of the blank, pressing out any air bubbles and smoothing it as best you can. (It may be helpful to wear gloves to avoid finger prints. If you have air bubbles, cut into the side of the bubble with your blade, press the air out and smooth.) Trim to the edges of the blank.

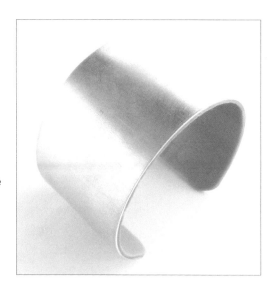

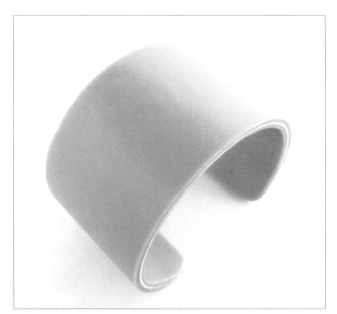

Roll another strip to a medium thickness (about 3 playing cards), and adhere it to the outside of the blank.

Remove any air bubbles as before, and trim the edges to match. Cover the edges by pinching the two layers of clay together and smoothing the edges .

Let rest for half an hour, then proceed to texture the upper surface with a ball-ended tool, tapping it all over in a close pattern and texturing the edge heavily.

Smooth over any spots where the metal becomes exposed if necessary. (Again, gloves are helpful to avoid fingerprints on the inside of the cuff as you hold it.)

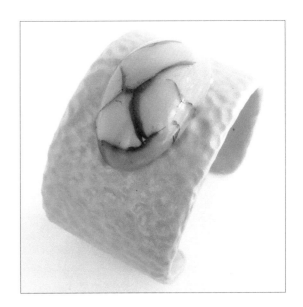

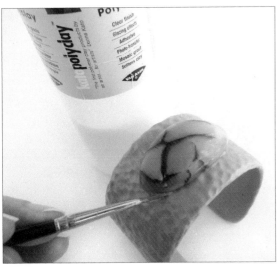

Step 3: Mounting the cabochon and forming the bezel

Apply a small amount of Polypaste to the bottom of the cab and make sure that it is centered in all directions. Place your cab onto the bracelet, and press down firmly.

Roll a sheet of clay to a medium thin thickness (about 2 playing cards) and cut a strip 1/8" wide, long enough to fit around your cabochon with some overlap.

Use your soft-bristled detail brush to apply a thin line of liquid clay all around the base of the cab where it touches the cuff.

Wrap your cab with the strip, overlapping the ends.

Trim at an angle (it is helpful to cut through both layers at once), and remove the excess.

Use your clay shaper tool to 'roll' the upper edges of your bezel close to the cab, smoothing and adjusting as you go.

Texture your bezel lightly to match the surface of the bracelet.

Check to make sure that the bottom of the bezel is seamlessly adhered to the cuff surface and smooth any gaps that you find.

Step 4: Coating and finishing

Using the 1/4" brush, apply a coat of the chosen metal to the bezel (it is easier to do small areas first), being sure to get the powder onto the very top surfaces of the bezel.

Wipe away any powder which may migrate to the cabochon surface with a damp clean brush or q-tip.

Using the larger brush, apply the metal powder to the rest of the bracelet. The inside is optional.

Clean the brush and use it to remove any excess powder. Examine for fingerprints; they can be removed by texturing over them with your ball tool.

Cure your bracelet at the recommended time and temperature.

Coat with a clear medium of your choice (See Primer—glazing).

If the cabochon has lost some of its luster in the curing process, either buff it again when cool, or glaze as you wish.

"Ha!" cried Peele, waving her bejeweled wrist under Parker's nose. "See, the metal inside allows me to bend this to just the right size —who would have thought that this material was so strong and yet so flexible?"

Studies in Ancient Limestone

Fossil Pebbles
Cycladic Goddess

My Dear Apprentice

Herein you will find the methods of creating ancient rocks from the antediluvian seas...

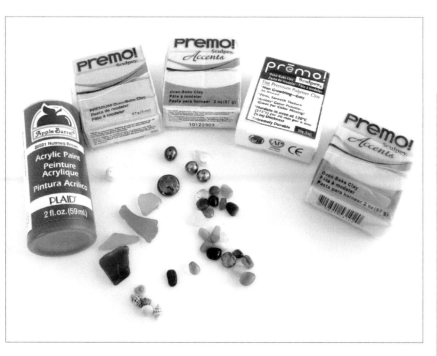

Fossil Pebbles

Supplies

Premo! polymer clay, 1 block each: White, Pearl, Translucent.

1/4 block Premo! Ecru clay

Shells, pearls, sea glass or other desired inclusions

Brown Acrylic paint

Liquid clay, such as TLS, (Translucent Liquid Sculpey) Fimo deco gel, Sculpey bake 'n' bond, or Kato Clear Medium

Tools

Tool Kit for Polymer Clay: See Primer —basic tool kit)

Textures: tiny sea shells, rough sandpaper, librarian's finger (recommended)

Stir straws

Sculpey etch 'n' pearl set *

Ball stylus *

Corn cob holder

*optional but highly recommended.

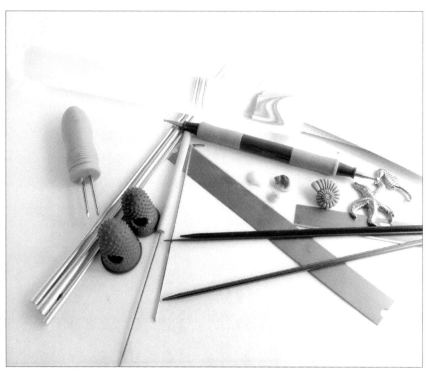

Step 1: Mix your colors

Condition all your clay until soft and pliable, divide each color in 4 parts. (See Primer— conditioning)

Mix 2 parts white +2 parts pearl

Mix 2 parts white + 1 part ecru

Mix 2 parts translucent + 2 parts pearl

Condition 2 parts pure translucent and set aside.

Mix combinations until almost blended, then roughly chop into pea-sized chunks. Sheet the pure translucent with the pasta machine, reducing the gap in the rollers a step at a time (See Primer —sheeting) until you have a very thin sheet; tear sheet into strips and bits.

Randomly mix the chunks and sheet. Break apart any uniform clumps.

Form into a loaf about 2" X 2" and roughly 4-5" long. Cut 1/4" thick slices from this loaf, and chop each slice up into small chunks again.

You should see a 'calico' effect on the surfaces of the loaf; if there are large areas of distinct color, chop the loaf up again and remix.

Step 2: Forming the shapes

Cut a 1/2" thick slice from the loaf and cut this slice into 4-6 pieces; form these into balls, then flatten into rough pebble shapes—have their purpose in mind; if they should be pierced through, keep them at least 1/4" thick. To suspend them from a jump ring, thin one edge. Experiment with a wide variety of shapes, just like natural stones

Step 3: Piercing

Many artists always drill the work after curing, but this is a matter of preference, and you may wish to pierce your work in the raw state. Let your work rest and cool down for at least 15 minutes before piercing.

If hanging your pebble from a jump ring, thin an area with your fingers and use your stir straw to create a hole. On an index card, Insert the straw into the clay, and twirl as you withdraw. Cut off the clogged end for multiple holes.

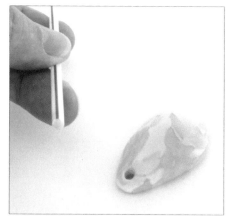

If you are piercing side to side, for parallel holes, mark your holes with a corn cob holder, and use a very thin needle to create a 'pilot hole': then follow the same path with a thicker needle to allow your cord or wire to pass freely; creating a pilot hole first minimizes distortion. When piercing, constantly twirl your needle as you are literally drilling through the raw clay. This keeps distortion to a minimum, and clean piercing is a good habit to acquire. Go through both sides to create a clear channel. Base the final hole on the size cord you wish to use for stringing.

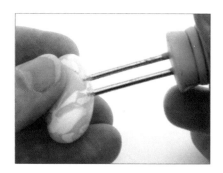

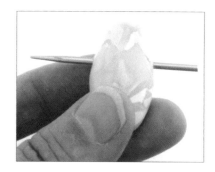

"AHHH!" cried Parker, almost dropping her clay. "That bloody needle went right for my finger tip!"

"Well, of course", murmured Peele, "that is precisely why you place your finger where you want the needle to emerge—it's instinctive."

Step 4: Embedding objects

If you wish to embed shells or other objects into your pebble, simply press your object into the soft clay until it is half covered but still visible. If your pebble is to be drilled all the way through after curing, your object must not interfere with the path of the drill. (Glass objects will stop and/or break a drill.) If you have pierced raw clay, do not press an object so far into the clay that it will crush the hole you worked to make.

Nearly any object but plastic can be safely embedded and cured into polymer clay. If in doubt, test by heating it in your oven for thirty minutes. Observe for heat damage; if there is none, it is safe to embed in clay.

Hint: Look through the floral and scrapbooking sections of craft stores for embeddable objects —crushed shell, gravel, no-hole glass beads, etc., all look great in pebbles.

Hint: the Sculpey Etch'n'Pearl tools are great for pressing tiny objects into the raw clay —the cupped end doesn't slip off rounded objects. This is also true for the flat end of bamboo skewers.

Step 5: Texturing

Texturing takes place in several stages. The marks you place on your pebble are a matter of preference, and it is useful to have a picture or an actual pebble nearby for inspiration.

Hint: place your work on an index card to facilitate ease of texturing and removal from the work surface. If you wish for the back of the piece to be textured, do that first.

On the first pass, use your librarian's finger or sandpaper to lightly texture all over the pebble. (The librarian's finger is preferable because it is light and easy to use and doesn't leave residue behind.)

On the second pass, pick out two or three small shells and impress their texture into the clay; experiment using different parts of the shell, grouping them loosely or tightly as you choose. You may also use buttons, stamps, anything that will make a shell-like impression.

Experiment! Remember if you are not pleased, you can roll up your pebble and do it over. Polymer clay is very forgiving.

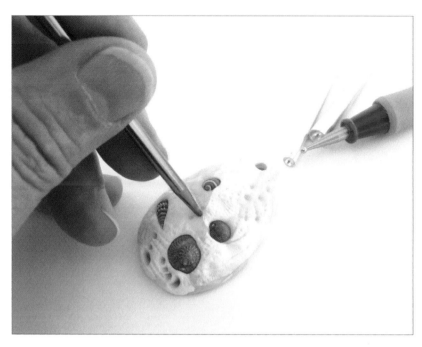

Hint: often a tight grouping of the same shell part looks more authentic.

On the third pass, use your Etch 'n' Pearl tools, ball stylus, double ended knitting needles, etc, to make random holes and indentations in your pebble. Experiment with depths and patterns, until you are pleased with the effect; think doodling. If you indent an area too deeply, either go over it with your librarian's finger again to 'erase' the marks, or add tiny blobs of fresh clay which you then re-texture. If it seems completely hopeless, pull out your inclusions and re-roll the clay into a new shape and do it again; never settle for less than you want.

Hint: Use your stylus to slightly push bits of clay over your embedded objects, both for authenticity and security.

Step 6: Curing

Cure your pebbles for the recommended time and temperature of the clay you are using, as stated on the package. (See Primer —curing) The curing process will bring out the both the translucence and the mica effect much more dramatically.

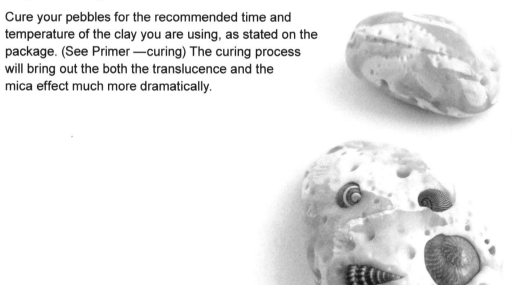

Step 6: Antiquing

Keep in mind that you are making something that looks as if it was long in the tooth before humans ever got their knuckles off the ground. A well-worn look is your aim. (See Primer —antiquing)

Pour out a blob of brown acrylic paint on your work surface. (A water bottle cap is a great container), and use a stiff brush to jam the paint into all your little crevices and impressions. Do one quarter of the surface at a time. (Acrylic paint dries fast.)

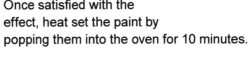

Apply the paint, count to five, then quickly wipe the surface of the work with a clean finger, baby wipe, or a damp cosmetic sponge. Take the color off the top but leave it in the depressions.

Do a section at a time, and gauge the effect; if you've applied too much, soak your pebble in cool water for a few minutes, then use an old toothbrush to scrub the paint out.

Once satisfied with the effect, heat set the paint by popping them into the oven for 10 minutes.

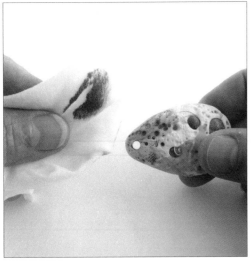

"Ah," said Peele, "look how perfectly the paint brings out all those cunning impressions that I made— really brilliant, if I say so myself."

So now that you have mastered the art of creating your very own Jurassic rocks, what do you do with them? Here are a few suggestions:

Step 7: Putting it all together

For bracelets, make sure your pebbles are thick enough to be pierced through the center and always two parallel holes to prevent flipping; if you have made a pebble that is too thin and later decide you wish to use it in a bracelet, add more clay to the back side (using liquid clay to assure a good bond), and pierce and texture as you wish. The final antiquing will hide the join.

For pendants, shape your pebble with one end no thicker than 1/8" and make a large hole so that it will swing freely on your jump ring or bail. You may also embed a wire into the raw clay, and then use pliers to form a connecting ring.

For earrings, embed an eye pin into the raw clay to connect with earring findings after curing. Alternatively, for a European look, embed a headpin into the raw clay, and shape the ear wire as you wish once the clay has been cured. Remember to sand the very end of the wire so that it slides smoothly though the earlobe.

For buttons, make sure your discs are the size of the garment hole, and use a corn-cob holder to make evenly spaced holes.

Cycladic Goddess Figure

My Dear Apprentice—

we may never fully decipher the mysteries of Ancient Minoan Civilization—its language and customs are all but lost. All we know for certain is that they revered the female form, as evidenced by their striking goddess figures, rendered in limestone. In them, the sacred feminine is realized in its simplest and most powerful form. Now that you have mastered the secrets of recreating limestone, here is how you may construct your own figurine:

Step 1: Shape the figure

Cut a thick slice of clay from your formed loaf—about 1/4" should do.

Roll this slice into a ball, then use your hand to roll it on your work surface into a tapered cylinder.

Use your knitting needle or other tool to press a channel deeply into the clay, about 1/2" from the thickest end.

Roll and press to create a smooth rounded channel.

Working on an index card, flatten the cylinder into a slightly rounded figure of pleasing proportions.

Take care not to obscure the separation between the head and body.

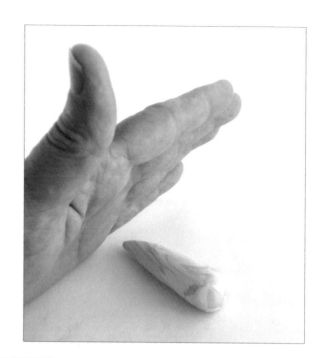

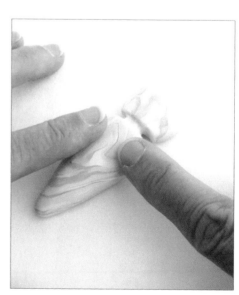

Step 2: Carve the lines

Once you are satisfied with the form, use the back of your cutting blade to impress lines into the top portion to suggest an arm crossing the waist.

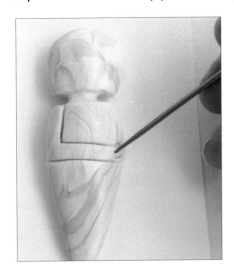

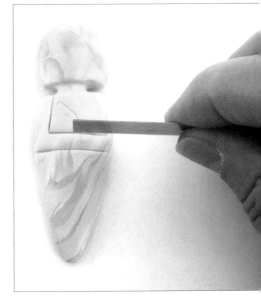

Use your knitting needle or other tool to form the lines of the fingers.

Texture the entire figure lightly with your librarian's finger or sandpaper.

Impress a line down the length of the body to suggest legs.

Peele looked up to see Parker holding her blade in the air with an anxious expression on her face; "Whatever is the matter, Noelia?"

Parker blushed, "She already looks so real—I feel as if I might hurt her if I press the blade too deep."

Peele rolled her eyes and sighed.

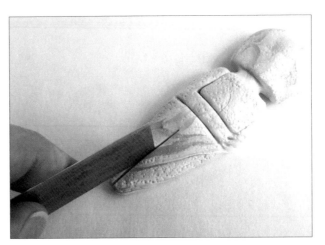

Step 3: Decorate the figure

Cut another thick slice from your loaf, cut off a strip, and cut this strip into tiny squares, which you roll into balls about the size of BBs. Cut these balls in half.

Use your Etch'n' Pearl tool to place these ball on the face of the figure in a pleasing pattern, perhaps suggesting corn rows.

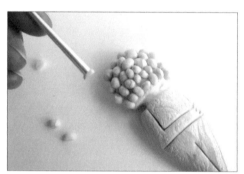

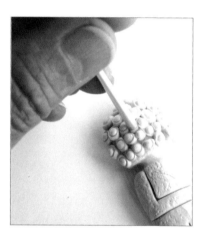

Use your smallest Etch 'n' Pearl (or a stir straw) to form circular indentations in the surface of each ball.

Use the pointed end to press a hole into the center of each circle.

Form a small snake of clay into a flattened strip, and drape it over the hips of the figure, cutting off each side with your blade close to the sides of the figure.

Use your Etch 'n' Pearl tool or stir straw to create a circular pattern along the strip.

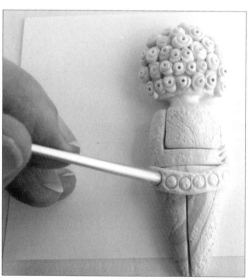

Roll tiny amounts of clay into thin strings, and curl these strings into spirals; place these on the chest of the figure, and if you wish, form a tiny double ended spiral to place on the leg for decoration.

Texture each addition as you go, and when all the elements are in place, proceed to texture as you did in the preceding exercise, using shells, and tools to create the fossilization.

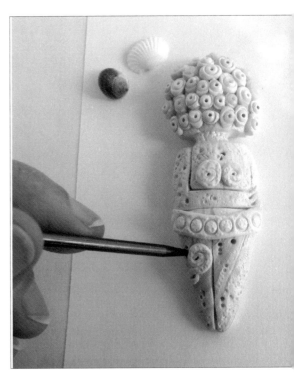

Step 4: Add a bail

Cure your work as previously, keeping in mind the greater time required for a larger mass of clay than a pebble. Roll a small amount of clay into a snake, and flatten this into a thin strip. Trim the long edges so that they are no wider that the 'neck' of your figure, then cut this strip to about 3/4" long.

Lightly texture the strip. Apply a very small amount of liquid clay to the back of your figure, then curving the strip slightly, position it on the back of the figure to serve as a bail for cord or chain.

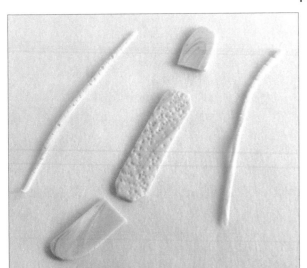

Check to make sure the gap is great enough to allow free passage. (You may use your knitting needle to raise it if necessary.) Use your stir straw or Etch 'n' Pearl to impress a decorative circle into each end of the strip where it joins to the body; this will insure a good bond.

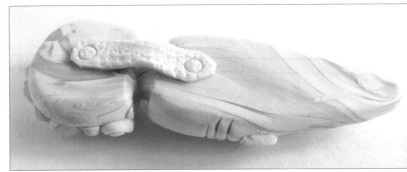

Step 5: Finish and String

Cure your figure again, face down so as not to crush your raw clay, this time for only 20 minutes or so; then proceed with the antiquing as previously discussed.

String your goddess as desired. A simple thong, or add shells, beads, pearls—the more rustic the better.

The version below shows scarabs made using a translucent clay tinted green and following the design in a later chapter. (See The Favrile Affair pg. 182) After curing, they were antiqued with white acrylic paint and buffed.

the Adventure of the Leopardskin Jasper

Primitive Pebble Bracelet

My Dear Apprentice

Jasper was the twelfth stone which adorned the breastplate of the high priest of the Hebrews, associated with the tribe of Benjamin. This particular variety—the loveliest of them all—is said to have very powerful healing properties. But I have chosen it merely for its beauty.

A note, My Dear Apprentice—mixing colors thoroughly accomplishes the process of conditioning, so why not save yourself a superfluous step?

Step 1: Mix the colors

For warm pink, mix 1/8 block of gold with 1/16 block of Alizarin Crimson, with 1/2 block Pearl.

For sage green, mix 1/8 block Blue Pearl with 1/4 block Gold with 1/4 block Pearl

For silvery grey, mix 1/4 block silver with 1/4 +1/8 block Pearl

Condition all of the black clay and the white clay. Sheet all the colors to a medium thickness (3 playing cards. See Primer—sheeting) and try to keep the sheets about 4" by 6".

Step 2: Build the stack

Beginning with the silvery grey, stack the sheets in this order:

Silver grey, warm pink, black, sage green, white.

Stretch sheets to fit if necessary, and lightly brayer each sheet before adding the next, to eliminate air bubbles.

Trim the edges and sides even on a medium thickness and set aside.

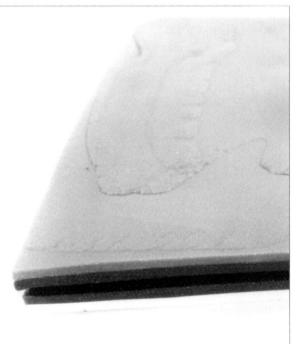

Supplies:
1/2 block Premo! Gold
1/16 block Premo! Alizarin Crimson
1/8 block Premo! Blue Pearl
1 1/8 block Premo! Pearl
1/4 block Premo! Silver
3/4 block Premo! Black
3/4 block Premo! White
Renaissance Wax (or other finish of your choice, See Primer —polishing)

Tools:
Basic tools for polymer clay (See Primer —basic tool kit for polymer clay)
1" circle cutter
Straight edge razors blades (optional but recommended)
Speedball Linoleum cutter with #3 (large line) blade
Sanding sponges or wet dry sandpaper in a variety of grits, the finest being at least 1000 grit (See Primer —polishing)

Step 3: Create the sheet

Using your hand roller or brayer, lengthen the stack until it is nearly thin enough to go through the pasta machine on a medium thick setting (4 playing cards).

Roll the stack through, then fold the white side to the inside and roll through again on the same setting. Fold and roll again.

Set the machine one step thinner to a medium thickness (3 playing cards. See Primer—stepping down) and roll the sheet through on a medium thickness (if necessary, cut the sheet in two pieces for ease of handling).

Step 4: Form the pebbles

Cut 1" circles from the sheet. Gather the scrap and roll it into snakes approximately 1/2" in diameter. Cut off 1/2" pieces of the snakes and roll them into balls.

Place the balls on the circles, and gather the clay up around the balls. It is not necessary to cover the core completely.

Roll the balls smooth.

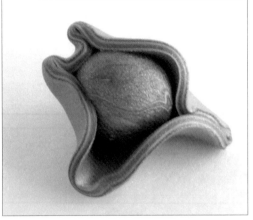

Step 5: Cut the surface

Observe your ball; there will be a bad side (seen on right—where the clay was gathered together) and a good side (seen on left—where the color should be a fairly uniform silver).

Cut only on the good side for the best patterns. When you cut into the 'bad side' the pattern reveals chaotic lines and squiggles.

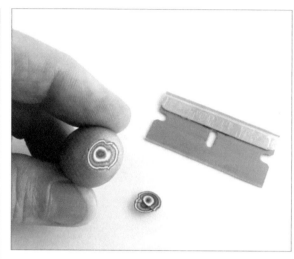

Using your sharpest blade (recommended is a straight edge razor blade) cut a small 'divot' off the surface of the ball by cutting straight across the curve

Observe the result —it should be a concentric ring pattern.

Deposit the divot onto the surface of the scrap clay sheet, or an index card.

Make more cuts, keeping them shallow, but experiment with different depths; if the cut reveals a pleasing pattern, continue. However, if the surface revealed is less than desired, you have two options:

Cut in the same place a trifle deeper, or use a pleasing divot to patch the area. As you work your way around the ball, use your 'good divots' to patch and cover the 'bad side'.

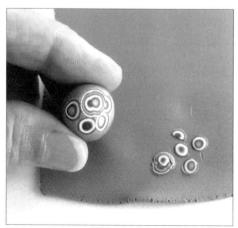

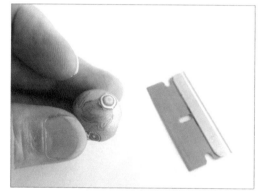

Extra divots deposited onto the scrap clay sheet and rolled smooth can be cut out and used to form new beads; they will not be exactly the same color as your original beads, but they will match because they were formed from the mass of clay.

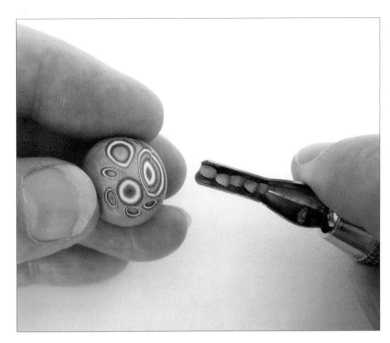

After making a few large cuts with your blade (try to keep these cuts no larger than 1/4" in diameter), use your Speedball #3 (large line) blade to cut very small divots between and around the larger cuts —this technique is different and requires more of a 'scooping' motion with the tool.

Experiment on scrap clay until you can make tiny divots with the linoleum cutter.

"I say, Nosie," observed Peele as she deftly whittled away at the clay in her hand. "This is ever so fun. You just never know what the cut will reveal; shallow, deep—they're all so different."

"So they are," agreed Parker, concentrating on the end of her linoleum cutter, "and once I've got the hang of this cutter it makes the most intriguing patterns."

Step 6: Form the pebbles and finish

After you have cut the surface as you wish, roll the ball smooth. Place on your work surface and use your fingers to gently form a pebble shape with a flat back. (Some flat areas on the surface look more authentic —use real pebbles as a guide.) Be sure to keep your pebble thick enough for stringing —no area should be less than 1/8" thick.

Smooth the pebbles to remove fingerprints. Cure at the recommended time and temperature (See Primer—curing) and let cool. Sand and polish, using a finish if desired (See Primer—polishing) Renaissance wax is the recommended finish.

Supplies:

Sufficient polished pebbles to form an 8" bracelet (number will vary depending on size)

Stretch cord (Stretch Magic 1mm recommended)

Hollow black rubber tubing or spacer beads (choice)

Tools:

Drill and bits (electric recommended, bits slightly larger than chosen cord)

Sharp side cutters

Arrowhead-shaped carving tool or bead reamer

Cyanoacrylate glue (optional)

Corn cob holder

Primitive Pebble Bracelet

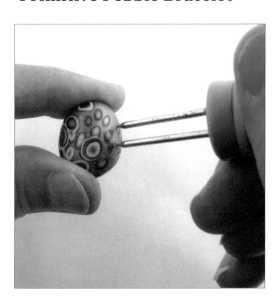

Step 1: Drill the pebbles

Use your corn cob holder to depress light marks into the side of your pebble bead, then drill through. Choose a bit which is slightly larger in diameter than the cord you will string the bracelet on. It is easier to hold the drill stationary and move the pebble to it, but use the method which suits you the best.

Midway through drilling, turn your bead so that you can make sure the line of the bit is parallel to the flat back.

If the drill is not long enough to completely pierce the bead, line up the hole visually and drill from the other side

until the two channels meet.

This will require some practice, so begin with your least -favorite bead. If you should drill through an area by accident, patch the hole with a small bit of translucent clay, cure for ten minutes and re-drill.

Please note, standard bracelet lengths run from 7 1/2" to 8". Measure your wrist to be sure by wrapping a strip of paper around it, mark and add about 5/8". Because your pebbles will vary in size, choose enough to fill this length with allowance for spacers between each; when you have strung all, check the fit before tying.

Step 2: String the pebbles

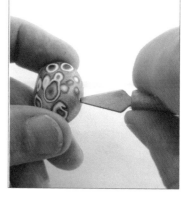

Cut two lengths of the stretch cord about 12-14" long. Cut the rubber tubing (if using instead of spacer beads) into very short lengths; about 1/16" to 1/8."

Lay your beads into a pleasing pattern. From whichever side you begin stringing, take the last bead and use your tool to ream out the holes on the outside slightly larger. This is where the knot will be concealed.

Begin stringing, using your spacers rubber or otherwise before the first bead. It may be necessary because of variations in size and thickness of the beads to adjust the length of the rubber spacers top and bottom. Pull snug occasionally to check the 'drape'.

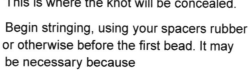

Alternate the beads and the spacers, checking for fit, and when you have strung both rows, pull the bracelet snug and check to see that the inner cord is concealed by the spacers. If not, adjust by restringing that area. See illustrations

When satisfied, take up the slack and tie three overhand knots in each cord, and make sure the knot is closest to the larger holes in the last bead.

Tie the first knot just enough to hold the bracelet snug, tie the second knot very tight, and the third knot very tight. The size of the knot should diminish enough to slip into the hole. You may wish to add a drop of the cyanoacrylate glue to insure the fidelity of the knot—this is optional.

Check for fit and admire!

Faux Twigs
Fantastical Forgeries Bracelet

My Dear Apprentice
We digress for an interval into pure fakery
for its own sake. Indeed, though by no means are
these items we are about to produce gems by any definition, yet there is a great benefit to the exercise. As a lesson
in sculpture, it sharpens the eye and practices the hand. The natural world practices deception daily, as every
butterfly that mimics the Monarch well knows, and it will be tribute to your skill to see how faithfully you imitate
the great imitator.

This also serves as an excellent practice of your drilling skills, for these twigs MUST be drilled after curing.
But you may also wrap them with wire, if you choose.

Faux Twigs

Step 1: Mix the colors and condition the clay

Mix 1/4 block of pearl with 1/4 block silver

Mix 1/4 block of pearl with 1/4 block white

Mix 1/4 block bronze with 1/4 block silver and 1/8 block black

Condition remaining 1/2 block of bronze

Form each color into a rough block and chop fine. Toss these tiny chunks like a salad, and reform into one rectangular block or loaf, about 1.5" by 3"

Supplies:

1 block's worth of scrap clay, mixed to a uniform color

1/2 block of Premo! Pearl

1/4 block Premo! White

3/4 block of Premo! Bronze (or Copper)

1/2 block Premo! Silver

1/8 block Premo! Black

Black and/or brown acrylic paint

Liquid clay or poly paste

Tools:

Basic tools for polymer clay (See Primer —Basic tool kit)

Modeling and sculpting tools (knitting needles, ball styli, Etch'n'pearl tools, etc)

Coarse brushes

Sponges or wipes

Step 2: Create the knothole or end cane

Cut a thick slice (at least 1/8") from your loaf, and roll through the pasta machine on a medium setting.(3 playing cards; See Primer —sheeting). Thin the resulting sheet down at least three settings thinner, one step at a time(See primer —sheeting) then fold once top to bottom and roll through again

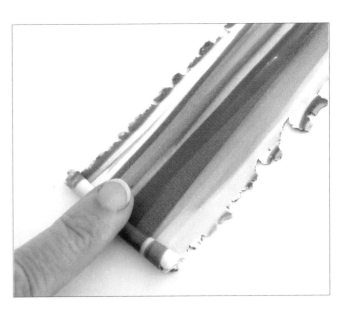

on the thin setting (About 1 playing card). Roll this sheet up tightly from one end to form a concentric ring or jellyroll pattern. Cut the roll in two and reduce one half (See Primer

—reducing) until it is twice as long. Cut this reduced half in two and reduce one half again. The goal is to create ever-smaller knotholes for your twig. The larger ones will be used to cover the ends. Keep cutting and reducing until you have a satisfactory assortment of sizes.

My Dear Apprentice

This random pattern we are creating—and there is more to come—is very subjective; if you feel the pattern is too large, simply cut up the loaf into chunks and remix; the pattern will grow small and finer. But keep in mind that we will mix it further.

One way to test the outcome is to cut a thick slice from the loaf as it is, and follow the subsequent instructions for the 'skin' of the twig in the fourth step; if the pattern revealed does not strike your fancy, then by all means, cut and remix the colors.

Step 3: Create the armatures

Condition your scrap clay (if necessary) and roll it into thin snakes. Cut these snake about the length of the desired twigs, and twist, pinch and form them into rough shapes.

Add small branches, keeping in mind that they may be worn against the skin and should therefore not be too 'spiky'.

Use your sculpting tools to further impress divots and creases into the clay; the skin or bark will soften these, so exaggerated features such as lumps and bumps are helpful.

When satisfied, cure at the recommended temperature for 15 minutes and cool.(See Primer —curing)

Coat each armature with a small amount of poly paste or liquid clay.

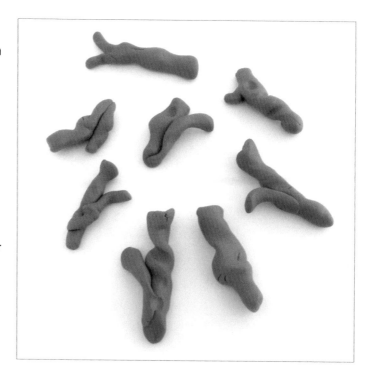

Step: 4 Create the skin or bark

Cut a thick (at least 1/8") slice from the loaf, and roll it through the pasta machine on a medium setting.(3 playing cards)

Step the pasta machine down one setting thinner and roll through again. Repeat.

Fold the sheet top to bottom and roll through again. Repeat this process, folding, rolling, and keeping the stripes vertical, until the colors begin to blend.

Cease whilst the stripes are still discernible but much softened. Step the pasta machine down one step thinner and roll the sheet through.

Rest the sheet on deli paper or an index card.

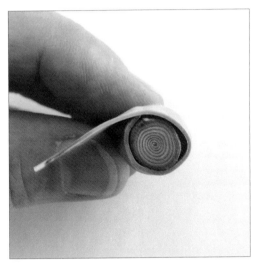

Step 5: Wrapping and smoothing

Begin to cover your twig by cutting slices from your larger knothole canes and covering the ends of the twig, pinching and shaping the knothole to the shape of the armature.

Cut thin strips from your 'skin' or bark, cutting across the colors and wrapping the armature 'mummy' fashion.

Overlap the strips and tear and patch as necessary, allowing the pattern to flow with the shape of the branches or other protrusions.

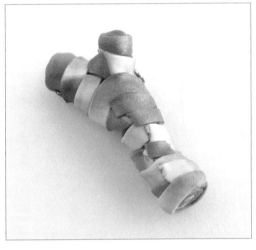

Wrap the skin or bark tightly to the end canes and smooth the seams. Use your fingers or sculpting tools to adhere the bark firmly to the armature in all places, depressing and releasing any air bubbles and working the clay deeply into all indentations and crevices.

Apply smaller knotholes now if you wish—they look most authentic on raised areas.

Smooth them to the skin with a blunt tool.

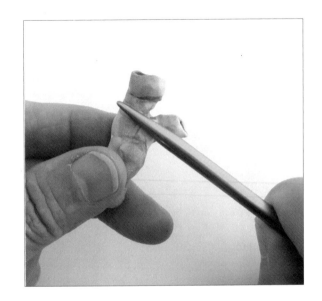

Step 6: Stippling and distressing the skin

Use your blunt ended sculpting tool or a fine ball stylus to begin stippling a pattern in the skin or bark. As a general rule, make these marks small and vertical, following the flow of the twig and varying the pressure, pressing and dragging to create different depths and lengths.

Think of small 'rivers' of marks meandering down the twig, then go back and fill the gaps between them, curving around knotholes and other protrusions for an authentic effect. When satisfied, go over the twig again with different tools, both fine and blunt to create distressed areas such as insect and bird damage: holes, fine lines, etc. For the final pass, use a blunt tool to create larger holes, tearing up the skin or bark slightly.

"Eeek!" cried Parker in alarm, "I've cut all the way down to the armature!" Peele gave her companion a wise look. "That's why you read the instructions ALL the way through, my dear; the holes and gaps will be disguised by the antiquing process. There's no need for repair; quite the contrary. Carry on."

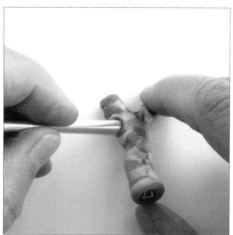

If desired, use your Etch 'n' pearl tools to accentuate the knotholes by pressing deeply in the center, then smoothing the outer rim with your fingers or other tools; an indentation in the center of this knob will look quite realistic.

When your twig is embellished to your satisfaction, use your sculpting tool to heavily pockmark the ends to suggest the rough grain of broken wood, if desired. (A smooth end will suggest deliberately cut wood.)

Cure all the twigs at the recommended temperature for at least 40 minutes, or more if the twigs are larger than 1/2" in diameter.

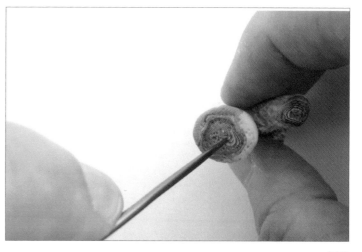

Step 7: Antiquing

Once cool, inspect your twigs; depending on the effect desired, you may wish to lightly buff the ends or high areas to suggest weathering, or smooth the portion of the twig which may come into contact with bare skin when worn.

For the final touch, antique your twigs with a wash of brown or black paint—or a combination of the two—using a coarse brush to jam paint deeply into the distress marks and crevices, and wiping the paint off the high areas with a damp finger or sponge.

As always, work in small areas at a time. (See Primer —antiquing) You may wish to heat set the paint by returning them to the oven for a brief (5 minute) period. No glaze is necessary unless desired.

"Now," sighed Parker, gazing at the collection of tiny branches in her hand, "whatever shall I do with them? I can't gad about in twigs like a savage, but they are so cunning I should really like to show them off."

"Grade school, " returned Peele, "make a bird's nest for your best hat! It's quite fashionable, I believe. Or, you could do as our forger suggests..."

My Dear Apprentice

By now you have mastered several techniques and must have a handsome assortment of extraneous oddments which you were not able to include in your other creations. What better use than to put them all into a bracelet?

The arrangement may be as higgledy-piggledy or formal as you choose, but I should say disregard convention and let your fancies run wild; you will surely be pleased with the result.

Supplies:

Faux twigs

Faux pebbles from other chapters:

Leopardskin Jasper

Opal

Bronze

Limestone

Elastic cord (Stretch Magic recommended)

Rubber tubing (pony bead lacing) or Sofglass tubing of at least 1 mm inner diameter

Cyanoacrylate glue

Tools:

Electric or hand drill with 1mm bit

Ball burr at least 2mm

Scissors or side cutter

Corn cob holder

Step 1: Decide the layout and drill the components

Most women's bracelets are about 8" in total length when laid out flat; if your wrist differs significantly, measure it by wrapping a strip of paper around it, marking the overlap and adding a little over 1/2".

Because of the variety of elements in this bracelet, it is important to arrange their order so that the different shapes 'nestle' into each other.

Take the time to try several configurations, keeping in mind that there will be spacers between them which will add to the overall length.

When you have decided on the best arrangement, mark your first element with the corncob holder and drill two parallel channels in it, coming back through the hole from both sides to insure clean channels.

Use the holes of the first piece to determine where to mark the next one —these holes may not necessarily be in the center, as with uniform elements. Be sure to clean all debris from the holes. When you come to the last element, use the ball burr on the outside holes to enlarge them; this is where the knot will be tied, and the larger hole will help the knots 'disappear'.

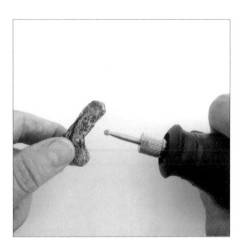

Step 2: String the elements

Cut two lengths of your chosen elastic at 12" to 14". String both the channels at the same time, as you will need to adjust the length of the spacers as you go—in many cases, the point of contact will not be the same for top channel and bottom channel.

It is worth your time to insure that the elements to 'hang' correctly.

Go slow and pull tight between each additional element to check the spacing.

The spacers will compress slightly and it is desirable to hide the stringing material as much as possible.

Adjust wherever necessary by cutting the spacer tubes longer or shorter.

Step 3: Finishing the bracelet

Once all of the elements are strung, place two spacers on the elastic cord protruding from the outside of first bead.

Gather the bracelet into a circle, and tie one overhand knot in one of the channels, being sure that the knot is next to the large hole in the last element.

Gently pull tight, taking up the slack in the bracelet and being careful not to 'bounce' the cord as you tighten. Steady pressure works best. (See the instructions for tying knots in the Leopardskin Jasper chapter pg. 102)

When all the slack is gone and elements and spacers are snug but not tight, proceed with tying your other knots. Pull these knots very tight to diminish their size.

You may wish to add a drop of cyanoacrylate glue on them for insurance. Trim the excess cords close to the knots and pull gently on the cords to urge the knots into concealment.

"My heart is always in my mouth," declared Parker, "as I tie that last knot. This clear string looks so frail, I am always sure it will break and scatter my work to the four winds."

"But as that hasn't happened," replied Peele smugly, "perhaps you'll let experience reassure you. It's the steady pull that's the key—keeps the string from rubbing up against the edges of the holes.

And the result I admit, is wonderful. It makes for a perfectly comfortable bracelet without the bother of fiddling with a clasp."

the Spell of Blue Lace

Blue Lace Agate Tile Bracelet

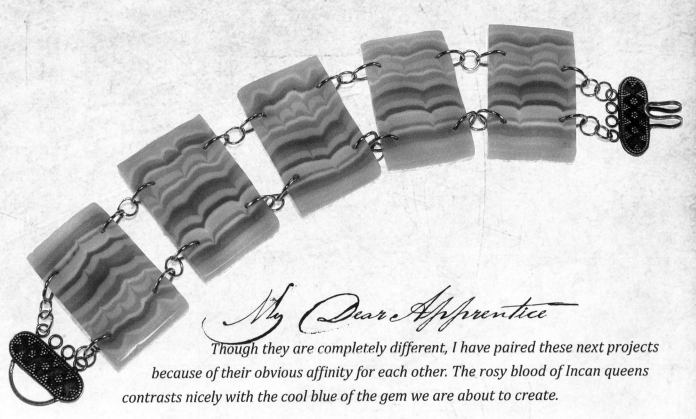

My Dear Apprentice

Though they are completely different, I have paired these next projects because of their obvious affinity for each other. The rosy blood of Incan queens contrasts nicely with the cool blue of the gem we are about to create.

Agates are very ancient talismans. Mentioned many times in the Bible, they are stones of protection; and in this case, of the means of communication. Blue Lace Agate is said to enhance the qualities of discourse, and more importantly, prevent a miss-spoken word. Especially important for us, in our endeavor.

Faux Blue Lace Agate Tile Bracelet

Before you begin, make a pattern of card stock 2 ½ by 3 inches.

Mix the following colors: (You will end up with five total; the mother color is used to make the rest)

Step 1: Mix the mother color

Condition and sheet the Ultramarine Blue to the thickest setting of the pasta machine and cut from it 3 ¾" dots. (See Primer—Measurements)

Mix these with 1/2 block of the White Translucent to a uniform color and sheet it to the thickest setting of the pasta machine.

Cut it as shown at right, into halves, and then one half into four parts.

Supplies:
¼ Block Premo! Ultramarine Blue

¼ Block Premo! White

3 ½ Blocks Premo! White Translucent

Card stock or index card

Tools:
Basic tool kit for polymer clay (See Primer—Basic tool kit)

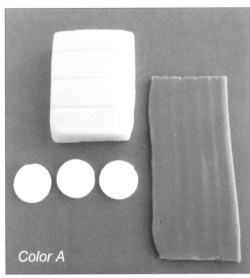

Color A

Use it to mix the following colors:'

Color A
½ of the square of mother color

1 block white translucent

3 dots white

Color B
½ block white translucent

3 of the quarters you cut from the mother color

Color C
½ block white translucent

The last quarter of mother color

Color D (The contrast layer)
½ Block white translucent

1 dot white

Color E
All leftover scrap from the sheeting process; you will have these scraps after sheeting the previous colors-

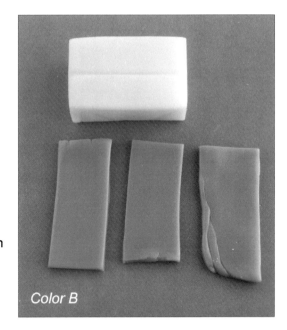

Color B

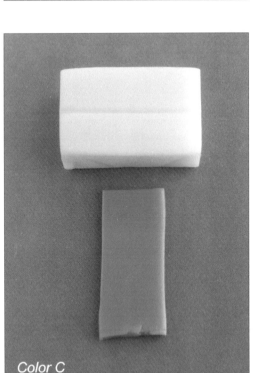

Color C

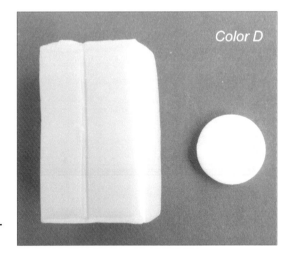

Color D

"All these lovely shades of blue," sighed Parker. "Not as bright as the bluebonnets in Spring, but it does remind me of the waters of Barton Springs. When we're finished here, what do you say to a swim?"

'The goal is to cut as many template sized rectangles as possible from each color of clay. When you have too little clay to cut a rectangle, set aside scrap for the Color E mixture.'

Step 2: Sheeting and assembling the cane.

Roll Color A to a medium thick setting on the pasta machine (4 playing cards). Using your cardstock template, cut out 2 rectangles. Roll remaining Color A to the medium setting on the pasta machine (3 playing cards).

Roll Color B to the medium thin setting of the pasta machine and cut rectangles as you did for Color A.

Re-roll scraps at the same setting and set aside any scraps.

Roll Color C to the medium setting on the pasta machine.

Cut and re-roll scraps as with the other colors, and set aside the remaining scrap.

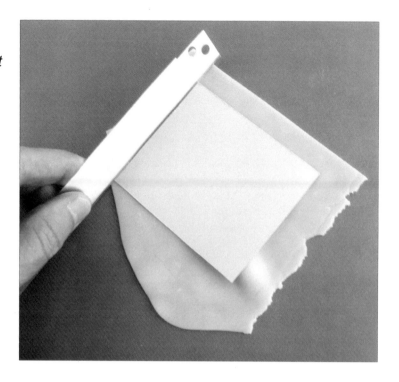

Roll Color D to a thin setting on the pasta machine, (1 playing card See Primer —sheeting) and set aside to cool for ease of handling.

Cut as many rectangles as you can. Set aside scraps.

Blend all the scraps into the last half block of white translucent.(this is color E)

Roll to the medium setting on the pasta machine.

Cut as many rectangles as you can. Gather the scraps and roll to a medium thin setting —one setting thinner—and cut additional rectangles.

Beginning with one of the thicker sheets of color A, stack rectangles at random, alternating colors for maximum contrast.

When you get four or five layers, distort the layers parallel to the short sides by pressing into the stack with the back of the clay blade wrapped in a sheet of paper. When you stack the next sheet, use a needle tool to gently press the clay into the grooves below.

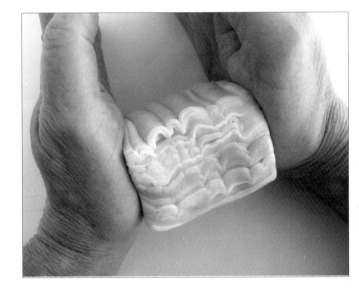

Continue to stack, stopping to distort the layers every fifth or sixth sheet until you have used up all the rectangles. Compress the block from the sides to make it taller and to further distort the layers. Allow block to rest for an hour or two.

"Well, now we know why our nemesis put these chapters together," observed Peele as she leafed ahead in the notebook, "it's almost exactly the same process; just different colors. Very thoughtful, that."

Blue Lace Agate Tile Bracelet

Step 1: Create the tiles

Using a very sharp, clean blade make 1/8 inch slices from the face of the block cane. Cut into one inch pieces.

Cure at recommended temperature for 30 minutes, and toss into ice water for maximum translucency. You will need 5 to 7 of these pieces, depending on the size of your wrist.(Measure your wrist by wrapping a piece of paper around it, marking the overlap and adding 1/2").

Sand and polish the tiles; you may leave one side—the inside—unpolished if you wish; this is more comfortable to wear.

On each long edge of the tiles, find the center and mark ½ inch from the center (Vertical axis), and 1/8" from the edge, for a total of four marks.

Use a pin vice or drill to drill a hole at each mark.

Supplies:

Blue lace agate block cane

3/8" jump rings

1/8" jump rings

Tools:

Flat Nose Pliers

Chain Nose Pliers

Sharp clay slicing blade

Drill or pin vise and 1/8" bit

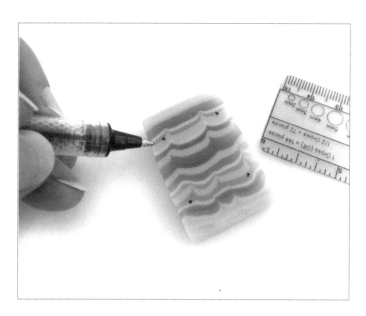

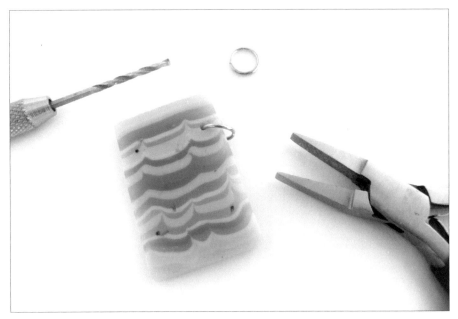

Using one set of pliers to hold the ring and one to twist, open the 3/8 inch jump rings and insert into each hole.

Join the tiles by linking the large jump rings together using the 1/8 inch rings.

Check the fit as you near the end and determine how many tiles you need, keeping in mind the total length of the clasp.

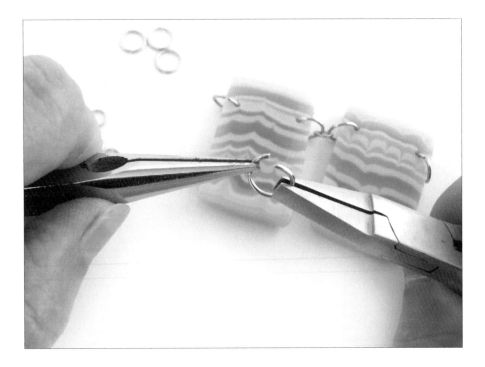

"I say, Parker," sighed Peele, grimacing as she twisted open yet another jump ring, "all these confounded tiny rings are really trying my patience—devilish hard to hold and go out of round if I look cross-eyed at them."

Parker smiled privately. "You know," she ventured, "it does help if you rest your wrists against the edge of the work-table. Brace your hands, as it were, whilst manipulating the pliers." For a moment silenced reigned. "What's that, Peele?"

"Mmmph," grunted Peele, "thanks."

Attach the clasp to the bracelet using the small jump rings; you may find that you need to use extra rings to get the correct 'hang'. If your bracelet is just shy of your needs, add more jump rings to make up the deficit.

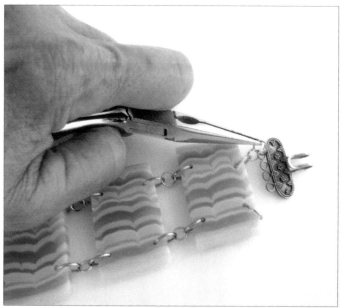

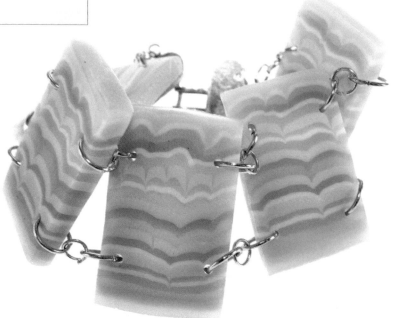

the Inca Rose Mystery

Faux Rhodochrosite Teardrops

Copper & Rhodochrosite
Tiered Necklace

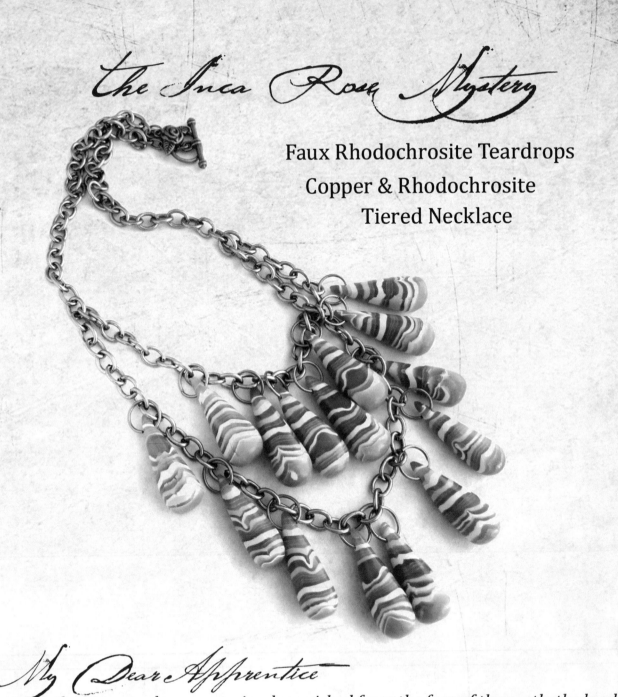

My Dear Apprentice

For the Inca people so mysteriously vanished from the face of the earth, the lovely pink gem you are about to create was the blood of their high-born queens, turned to stone; for that reason it is known as the Inca Rose. Such a macabre thought, no?

Step 1 : Mixing the colors

Color A: 2 blocks of Translucent cut into slices; add to this 4 3/4" dots of Alizarin rolled on the thickest setting of the pasta machine (9 playing cards).

Blend until uniform (this also conditions your clay). Set aside. Most of the other colors will be blended from this.

Color B: 1/2 block Translucent plus 1" strip of Color A approximately 6" long rolled to the thickest setting of the pasta machine.

Color C: 1/2 block Translucent plus 2" strip of Color A approximately 6" long rolled to the thickest setting of the pasta machine.

Color D: 1/2 block of White mixed with 1.5" square of Ecru rolled to the thickest setting of your pasta machine.

Color E: Take 1/2 of Color D and mix into it a 1" by approximately 6" strip of Color A.

Supplies:

1 block Premo! White clay

3 blocks Premo! Translucent clay

Small amount Premo! Alizarin Crimson clay (about 1/4 block)

Small amount of Premo! Ecru clay (about ¼ block)

Ivory acrylic paint

Tools:

Basic tools for polymer clay—See Primer, Basic tool kit

Small knitting needle

Stiff Blade

Cardstock cut to 3" X 4" inches (template)

3/4" circle cutter

Step 2: Make the sheets

Starting with color A, (thickest setting) cut to the 3"X4" template; then re-roll the scraps into successively thinner sheets of clay to cut as many squares of this size as possible. Lay these sheets on a surface which can be painted without harm. Repeat this process with colors B and C. Paint these sheets with a thin layer of the Ivory acrylic paint, leaving one sheet unpainted for the top of your stack, and set the painted sheets aside to dry.

While these sheets dry, cut colors D and E using your template, starting out at a setting 2 settings thinner than colors A B and C, and re-rolling the scraps into thinner sheets for each successive cut.

Save aside a small amount of the scrap and roll into a snake about 3" long by 1/4"; take all of your remaining scrap and blend into a sheet which you can cut using the template.

Step 3: Assemble your block.

Note: this technique depends upon a fairly random assembly of the stack, so long as contrast is maintained.

Begin by stacking 3 or 4 sheets of different colors and thicknesses, painted side up. Using your knitting needle, distort the clay by pressing deeply into the sheets staying parallel to the short side of the stack and spacing the indentations randomly. Add three of four more random sheets, and distort this layer with a blade wrapped in a sheet of paper.

Continue adding and compressing subsequent layers, distorting with your needle and blade.

When you reach the halfway mark, add in your snake, placing it into a deep depression.

Continue to add and distort sheets at random, stopping occasionally to compress the stack and force out any air bubbles.

Remember to finish with an unpainted sheet.

Step 4: Reducing the cane & forming the drops

While the block is still warm, reduce in height until about 3/4" (This is just to size the beads and keep the waste to a minimum.)

Cut a 3/8" slice from the face of the cane, and cut this slice into rectangles about 3/8" by 3/8".

Starting about halfway down the piece, shave off the corners to produce a teardrop shape.

Roll gently until smooth.(For more variety occasionally shave your beads from the opposite end.)

Hint: to help achieve the rounded end, use your hand roller or other tool to smooth it. Do not fret about making them all the same; a variety of sizes and shapes adds an air of authenticity.

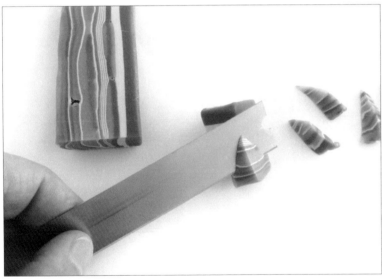

"See," murmured Noelia, "I told you so. Stop measuring!"

Let the drops cool slightly, then pierce them side to side a little less than 1/4" from the narrow tip. Try to avoid distorting the ends.

Hint: save your shavings and scrap for other beads

Cure at the recommended temperature for at least 30 minutes, and drop into ice water straight out of the oven to increase the translucency.

Inspect for fingerprints, sand to 2000 grit and polish. (see Primer—Polishing.

My Dear Apprentice

A small note; rounded beads roll, do they not? But there is a simple solution: merely fold an index card accordion-fashion, and Voila! You have a perfect curing rack for your lovely beads.

Tiered Copper & Rhodochrosite Drop Necklace

Step 1: The jump rings

Make 15 jump rings using the 18 gauge copper wire by winding the wire around the knitting needle or dowel about 19 times.

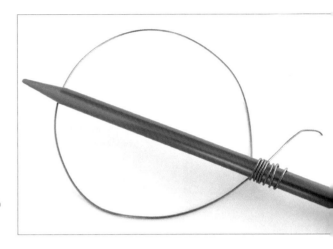

Cut jump rings apart with the wire cutters, sanding the edges flush if necessary.

String your drops onto the rings.

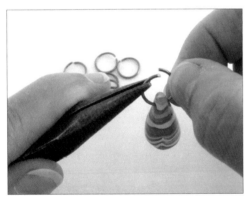

Supplies:

15 finished rhodochrosite drop beads

Copper oval link chain (choice)

Copper clasp (choice)

12" of 18 ga copper wire

Liver of sulfur

Tools:

3/8" diameter dowel or knitting needle

Wire cutters

Jewelry pliers (chain nose recommended)

Peele grumped, "Nosie, how the devil are you getting your rings back together and still round? Mine have gone all wobbly..."

Parker gave her companion a deprecating smile, "Grade school, dear girl; don't pull the ends of the ring apart—simply hold the closed ring in your fingers, use the pliers to twist the ends away from each other sideways, string your bead onto it and twist the ends back together."

"Hmpph!" retorted Peele, after completing this maneuver successfully. "Easy when you know how."

Step 2: Attach to the chain

For the lower tier, measure 21 ½ " of copper chain. Find the center of the chain and attach the first drop with a jump ring. On each side of the center drop, skip two links of chain and attach another drop.

Skip three links and attach another drop, repeat. Then skip four links and attach one more drop. Now, attach the upper tier to the necklace. Skip three links from the outside (last) drop, and attach to one side a 6 3/4" piece of chain. Repeat for other side.

Find the center of the upper tier and mark it with a thread or a twist-tie.

From this link, skip one link and attach a drop. Skip two links and attach another drop. Skip two more links and attach another drop. Repeat for other side.

The upper tier should have a total of six drops, the lower tier a total of nine. Measure the necklace by holding it around your throat and look in a mirror.

Step 3: Attach the clasp and finish

Decide the length you prefer and attach your clasp.

Following package directions for the liver of sulfur, patina your necklace (if desired), checking it occasionally for depth of color—liver of sulphur turns copper black for an aged look. (The liver of sulfur will not affect the clay drops.)

When your chain reaches the desired depth of patina, drop it into a bowl containing a bath made from 2 cups of water and 3 tablespoons of baking soda to neutralize the chemical reaction, rinse in plain water and let dry.

"Phew!" cried Parker, holding her nose and fanning vigorously, "That chemical bath positively reeks of rotten eggs!"

"Indeed," agreed Peele, "We really should have done this outside—well, lesson learned. But isn't it a lovely color?"

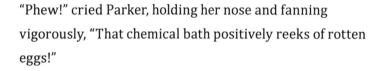

Qin Dynasty Bangles

My Dear Apprentice—

Jade is the most revered of ancient stones, durable enough to be made into weapons, beautiful enough to grace the arm of an Imperial consort. Always given as a gift—never purchased—should it break, be assured it has sacrificed itself to protect its wearer from great harm.

Qin Dynasty Bangles

Step 1: Preparation

Condition all your clay. (See Primer —Conditioning) Keep colors separate and be sure not to confuse translucent and white Using half of the white clay, roll a sheet on the second thickest machine setting and set aside. You will use it to wrap your cane later.

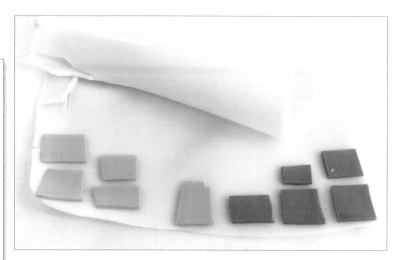

Supplies:

3 blocks Premo! Translucent polymer clay

Small amounts of Premo! Green and Yellow clay (choice) 1/4 block total

1 block Premo! White polymer clay

1 block's worth of scrap clay —any dark color

Pasta machine

Tools:

Work surface

Pasta machine

Craft blade/tissue blade

Acrylic roller

Baby wipes

Bracelet form: soda can, biscuit/circle cutter.

Baking surface: tile, cardboard, etc.

Disposable examining gloves (optional)

Wet/dry sandpaper in grits from 400 —1200

Renaissance or other fine paste wax

Hint: clean your pasta machine rollers frequently, especially between color changes. Baby wipes are perfect. Press hard on the bottom of the rollers—that's where most of the cross contamination takes place.

Step 2: Tint the Clay

Roll half of your translucent clay into a long sheet on the thickest setting, and tint it: roll your green and yellow clays to a medium setting (3 playing cards) and cut roughly half-inch squares; five of each color should do.

Place these squares at the bottom of the translucent sheet, more squares on the outside and fewer toward the center —-tinting is not an exact science, so you can always add in more color if you wish. It is best to start light, as taking color out is more difficult.

Step 3: Make a blend

Roll this sheet through the pasta machine on the medium setting (3 playing cards), keeping the stripes vertical, and fold it top to bottom (like colors together). Roll through again. Continue folding and rolling until the colors blend seamlessly; this is a basic gradient blend. (see the Primer —Skinner Blend)

Once the colors are blended to your satisfaction, turn the sheet so that the fold is to one side, and roll through the machine to elongate the blend. Thin your sheet by stepping down your pasta machine (see Primer —Reducing) until you reach a medium thin thickness(about 2 playing cards). Set this long blended sheet aside.

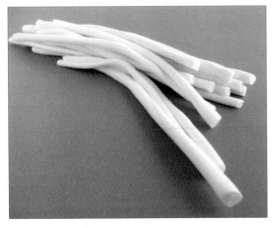

Step 5: Make the bullseye cane

Form the remaining untinted translucent clay into a short log about 4 inches long and wrap evenly with the sheet of white that you rolled to the second thickest setting; trim the ends to abut, and smooth the seam. Set aside the remaining white clay.

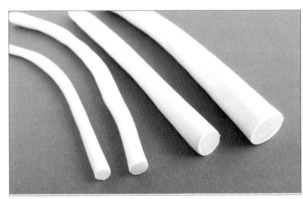

Reduce this log—a bull'seye cane—to a snake about 12" long. (See Primer—reducing)

Cut in half, reduce each half to 12" again, then continue to cut and reduce all pieces until the resulting snakes are about the diameter of a bamboo skewer. Cut each to the width of the colored sheet.

"Oh look," cried Parker with delight, "Papa bear, Mama bear, baby bears..."

Step 6: Build the cane

Lay out your long tinted sheet on a clean work surface, and lay your thin translucent/white snakes evenly along the length., trimming to fit. Save your discards to patch where necessary

Press the snakes gently into the sheet, then cut the sheet in half and lay one on top of the other so that the yellow rests on the green, and the snakes are spaced between each other.

Press with your fingers or other tools to remove air pockets and slightly flatten the 'sandwich'.

Roll both ends toward the center, one at a time. Go slow and compress to remove air bubbles as you roll; you may use a knitting needle or other tool to compress the sheet next to the snakes.

(The clay may crack —this is normal and no cause for worry. When both ends have been rolled up, compress and flatten your cane into a long rectangle, squaring and smoothing it.

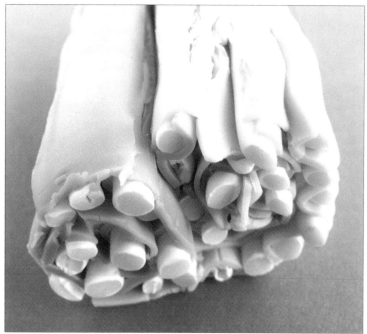

Step 7: Reduce

Starting at the center, reduce this log by pinching and gently stretching until it is about twice as long as it was originally. Use your hand roller to keep the sides smooth and even.

Hint: gently twisting and then returning to center is a fast easy way to reduce a squarish cane like this one. As it warms the reduction speed will increase.

Step 8: Stack the cane

Cut this log in half and line up the cut ends into a pleasing pattern. This is a 'mirror' cane. Press the two canes together and reduce again, until it is once more twice as long as the original. Cut in half and stack one on the other in a pleasing pattern.

Experiment with different configurations of the matching sides; it's amazing how different the pattern can look by flipping the sides.

After you have determined your pattern, reduce again, keeping the shape of your cane rectangular and lengthening by only a few inches this time. Let this final reduction rest for at least an hour before cutting slices from it.

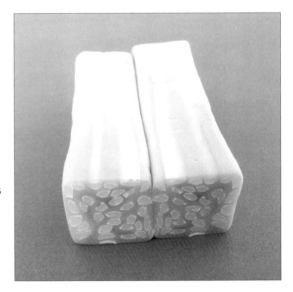

Step 9: Make the bracelet core and skin

Condition your scrap clay until pliable, and roll into a snake a little more than 1/4" in diameter and about 12" long. Sheet the remaining scrap to a medium thin thickness, and cut a strip about 12" long and 1 and 1/2" wide.

Cover this strip completely with canes slices applied randomly; multiple layers will result in great depth. Roll smooth with your roller or brayer. Straighten the long edges by trimming. Don't be neat; overlap the slices—the pattern will show through.

Hint: to cut paper thin slices, start from the center of the cane 'face' not the edge, and 'wiggle' your blade; wiping the blade frequently with a baby wipe is very helpful.

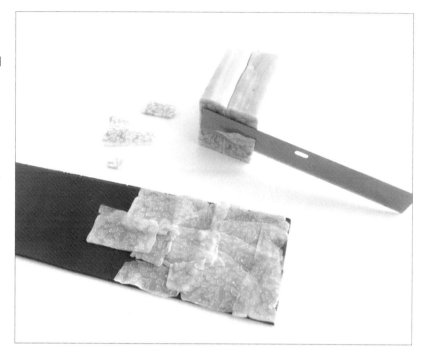

Step10: Cover the core

Working on a sheet of paper, flip the strip over so that the scrap side is up. Place the scrap snake on it and bring up the sheet to cover the snake; Pinch the tinted clay over the seam, and patch if necessary to conceal the core. Roll smooth without lengthening, and make sure the ends are close in size.

135

Step 11: Form the bracelet

Form your bangle around your chosen form; soda cans, glass jars, and circle cutters are all workable. To determine the size of your wrist, wrap a strip of paper loosely around it, mark, and add 1/2" to 3/4", depending on how snug a fit you like. You may also determine which form fits best by slipping an existing bangle you wear onto it; if it fits, the form is the right size.

Using gloves (recommended), wrap your snake snugly around the form, overlapping the ends. Use your blade to cut down through the snakes at an angle to form a 'lapping' joint. This is stronger than a straight vertical cut.

Apply a tiny amount of liquid clay to the cut ends, join, and smooth the seam carefully with your fingers, trying to avoid distorting the clay. (Once you have smoothed the inner seam, you may wish to slide your bangle onto the form and finish smoothing the outside edges. You may leave the bangle on the form for curing if you wish.

If not, form your bangle into your desired shape—many people prefer ovals for comfort—and place it on your curing surface.

Hint: If you trace the outside of your form onto cardboard, you have both a shape guide and a curing surface in one.

Step 12: Cure

Cure according to the manufacturer's directions; (Times and temperatures are on the package) Always use an oven thermometer! Immediately after removing from the oven, slip into a bowl of ice water. (This increases translucency.)

Step 13: Finish

When completely cool, examine for divots or other imperfections. If they are deep, scrape some translucent clay into them, smooth, and cure again for 20 minutes.

If sanding is necessary, begin with very fine wet/dry sandpaper—400 grit or finer and proceed through the grits until you reach 1200. Buff with a coarse cloth to bring up a shine. You may wish to apply a fine paste wax, such as Renaissance Wax.

Let dry to a haze, then buff vigorously with a soft cloth. The examples show how the same cane looks over different core colors, light and dark. Feel free to experiment!

My Dear Apprentice

Amber, that most ancient and delightful of natural gems, is also admirably suited for fakery; especially in this marvelous medium we have at hand. Used for millennia in jewelry, medicine, and perfumes, it was even wrought into an entire palace room for the benefit of the Russian Czar, Peter the Great. The eighth wonder of the world, it is said. We shall content ourselves with a less ambitious but no less beautiful project—a Turkmen necklace such as a princess of the Steppes would have worn.

the Scent of Amber

Caravan Necklace

Caravan Necklace

Step 1: Create the colors

Divide the block of translucent into fourths. Sheet each of the five quarter blocks to a medium thin setting on the pasta machine.(2 playing cards; See Primer —Sheeting)

Tint each sheet according to the following formulas by smearing the ink on the sheet, allowing to dry, then folding and rolling on the same medium thin setting until the colors are nearly uniform; a little streakiness is desirable.

Sheet One: 10 drops Latte

Sheet Two: 9 drops Caramel

Sheet Three: 2 drops Sunshine Yellow and 2 drops Ginger

Sheet Four: 2 drops Sunshine Yellow and 6 drops Ginger

Sheet Five: 3 drops Sunshine Yellow and 2 drops Burro Brown.

"Hmm," frowned Peele, holding up her sheets of clay to the light, "I'm not sure I'm entirely delighted with these colors."

"Oh, don't worry!" replied Parker. "Remember, translucent clays get much richer and clearer with curing—you'll see."

(These amounts of clay are calculated to make enough beads for the Caravan Necklace. If you wish to make extra for other projects, simply multiply the number of drops per quarter block increase that you need.

For example, if you wish to double the amount of the first color, add 20 drops of Latte to 1/2 block translucent).

Clay Sheet Supplies:

Ranger Adirondack Inks in the following colors: Latte, Caramel, Sunshine Yellow, and Ginger

Jacquard Pinata Ink in Burro Brown

1 ¼ blocks Premo! Translucent (Note: regular Translucent)

Tools:

Basic tools for polymer clay (See Primer—Basic tool kit)

Supplies:

Amber tinted clay sheets

3/8" brass compression sleeves (available in the plumbing section of home improvement stores.)

1/4 block each Premo! Black and Gold

White glue

Waxed cotton cord (black recommended)

20 gauge copper wire

S hook for clasp (or you may forge your own—see instructions)

Renaissance Wax

Tools:

Rubber tipped clay shaper or knitting needle

Side cutting pliers

Round nose pliers

Chain or flat nose pliers

Needle tool

Liver of sulphur

White glue

Jeweler's hammer and bench block (if forging your own clasp—optional)

Step 1: Create the beads and elements

Fold each of the tinted sheets into quarters. Cut these quarters into four pieces, for a total of 20 pieces. (There will be about 8 leftovers, if you wish to make the necklace longer than illustrated)

The size of the beads is a matter of preference; they may vary. Form the beads by rolling smooth balls, then shape into a flattened oval, a little less than ¼ inch. Use the needle tool to make a hole in the center. With the clay shaper or other tool, enlarge the hole to a generous 1/8" and smooth the edges of both sides of the hole. Make at least 10 of these beads. (a few divots or scratches on the surface of your disk makes it appear more authentic).

Tip: A small square of craft foam sheet makes a perfect surface for piercing beads.(available in the children's section of the craft store)

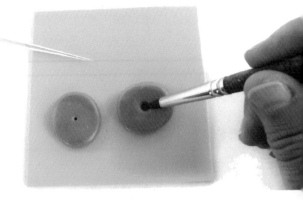

To make the focal bead, take two of the pieces of clay (Two different colors lightly mixed are intriguing).

Roll into smooth ball and then into a snake about 3/8" in diameter. Pull each end into a point. This should be around 3" in length. Curve into a semi-circle.

Note: to give the compression sleeves an aged patina, place in a small plastic container, cover with full strength household ammonia, cover and set aside for about 3 days. Rinse and let dry.

Step 2: Filling the brass compression sleeves.

Mix black and gold clay to make a dark bronze color. Roll into a log 3/8" in diameter. Slide a compression sleeve onto the log and slice down through the clay, leaving a bit extra on each side. Pinch between your thumb and forefinger to press the clay firmly into the sleeve. Pierce a hole in the clay. 4 strands of the cord will pass through this hole, so enlarge it by rotating the needle tool in the hole. (This also pushes the clay into the ridges of the sleeve so that it will stay secure.) Trim any excess. Prepare 14 of these clay and brass beads.

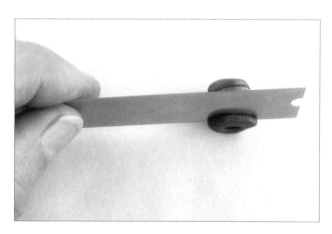

"Well", observed Parker, rolling the brass beads in her palm; "they certainly do look ancient with that cloudy patina; who would have thought that simple ammonia would do all that?"

Cure all beads at the recommended temperature for at least 30 minutes. (See Primer—curing). After removing the smaller beads, return the focal element to the oven for another 15 minutes as its larger mass requires more time.

Step 3: Finishing the elements

Sand all of the amber beads. Use 400, 600, 800 and 1000 grits of sandpaper. Apply Renaissance wax, let dry for a few minutes and apply a second coat. When dry, buff with a soft cloth. Buffing on an electric wheel is not recommended as it makes the beads too shiny. The wax finish makes them look more 'real'.

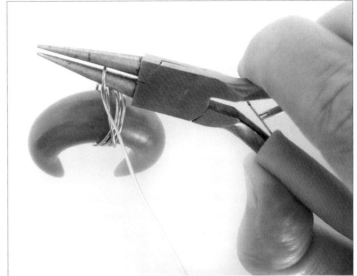

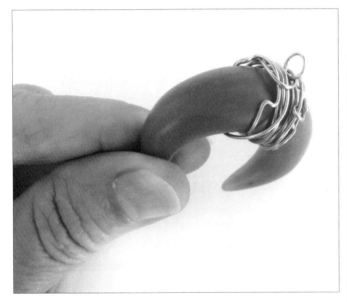

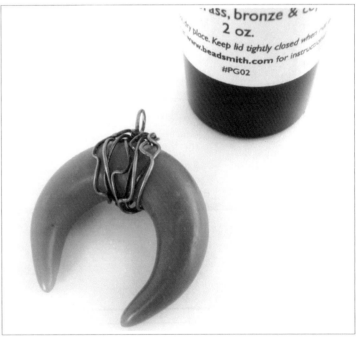

To finish the focal bead, using an 18 inch piece of 20 gauge copper wire and starting in the center of your bead, wrap the wire around the bead five times. With the round nose pliers form a hanging loop large enough to accommodate 4 strands of your cord. With the remaining wire, wrap around the bead four or five more times, tucking the end under the wraps. Clip off the extra wire as close as you can. Using the chain nose or flat nose pliers make several crimps in the wires by gripping a strand with the pliers and giving it a small twist. This tightens up the wires and adds interest. Patina the wire using the liver of sulfur according to the package directions.

Step 4: Stringing and finishing.

Cut four strands of waxed cotton cord, about twice the length of your desired necklace. (To make stringing easier, divide the cords into pairs and add a dab of white glue to the ends of each pair.)

String the focal bead onto all four cords. On either side, string two compression sleeve beads, also on all four cords.

Begin adding the amber beads by bringing one pair of cords through from the top and one pair up through the bottom.

Add a compression sleeve bead on all four cords. Continue until you have added five amber beads, with a brass bead between each one, ending with one of the brass beads. With all four cords tie an overhand knot next to the last brass bead

"This is rather like sewing," said Peele, "not, of course, that I would know anything about that."

To finish the ends, use an eight inch length of 20 gauge wire. Form a quarter inch loop about 1 inch from the end and wrap the loop once, using the shorter end of the wire.

Make a U-shape with the long end of the wire, just under the wrapped loop. Fold the cords in half, about two inches from the last bead and catch the cords in the wire.

Add a drop of white glue between the folds of cord for extra security. Tightly wrap the remaining wire around the cords a few times, clip off ends of cords and wrap a couple more times. Repeat on the other side. Add the S-hook to one side.

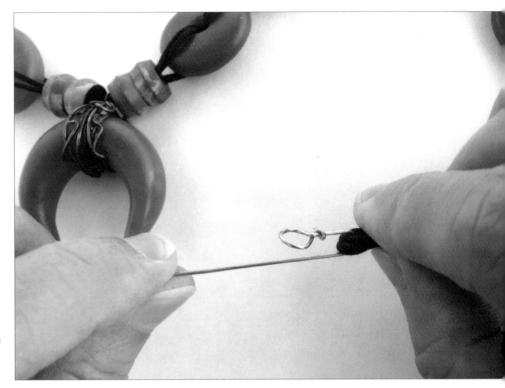

Note: you can easily hand forge your own S-hook. Simply make two opposing loops, using an approximatly 3" piece of wire. Clip off the wire about 1/8 inch past where the loops cross the center. Curl back the tips. Lightly hammer your hook with the round end of the jeweler's hammer on the bench block. This adds texture and work hardens the hook so it will be very strong.

"Now, here's the stuff," gushed Parker, hammering away at the wire. "I can consider myself a regular blacksmith now!"

Peele glanced over, and for once thought the better of what she was about to say.

the Primeval Coral Caper

Petoskey Stone
Rock Hound Necklace

My Dear Apprentice—

We now move to an obscure but very beautiful stone discovered quite recently in the young state of Michigan. It is Devonian coral, fossilized eons ago, but named for a famous chief of the Ottawa nation—Petosagey, or Rays of the Dawn. In its natural state, Petoskey stone is quite plain, but once polished it is lovely beyond belief, and one of the few American gems to honor its native inhabitants.

Note: Fossilized coral is found in myriad shades of grays, beiges and browns. Three different formulae are offered here; that which you make is up to you. Each formula will take a whole block of translucent, mixed with varying small amounts of the other listed colors to form a cane that holds the pattern; should you desire to make all three, please obtain 2 more blocks of Premo! Translucent. Where 'dot' is referred to, that is a 3/4"circle cut from a sheet rolled to the thickest setting of the pasta machine (9 playing cards See Primer— sheeting) Again, keep in mind that mixing colors also accomplishes conditioning.

Step 1: Mix the colors

Formula One:

For the inner color of the cane mix ½ block of translucent with one dot of black plus one dot of raw sienna. Blend thoroughly with your pasta machine and set aside.

For the outer color of the cane mix ½ block of translucent, ¼ block white and 5 dots of black. Blend and set aside.

Formula Two:

Inner color- Mix ½ block of translucent with 1 dot of black.

Outer color-Mix ½ block of translucent and ¼ block white, plus three dots black and one dot raw sienna.

Formula Three:

Inner color- ½ block translucent with one dot raw sienna

Outer color- ½ block translucent with ¼ block white, two dots black and one dot raw sienna.

Supplies:

1 Block Premo! Translucent

1 Block Premo! Black

1 Block Premo! White

1 Block Premo! Raw Sienna

Tools:

Basic tool kit (See Primer —basic tool kit)

  3/4" circle cutter

  Dowel or large knitting needle

Formula Three

Formula Two

Formula One

Step 2: Form the canes

Form inner color into a cylinder about 1" in diameter by 1 1/2" tall. Flatten the sides of the cylinder to a point. Using a knitting needle or dowel rod about 3/8" in diameter, press opposite the point to form a rounded channel.

With the rod in the channel, pull the edges around the round to thin and elongate them as shown.

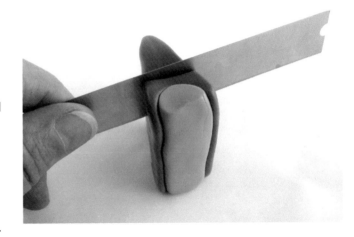

Roll a 3/8" log of the outer color and reserve the rest of this color. Press the log into the channel, and flatten the back of the log on your work surface.

Use your clay blade slice to through the shape from top to bottom, about ¼ inch away from the rounded side of the log.

Sheet the remaining outer color to a medium thickness on the pasta machine (3 playing cards). Place the section with the inner and outer color on a small piece of this sheet and trim to fit, then rejoin them so that there is now a line of the outer color between the cylinder and the rest of the triangle.

Take your remaining outer color and wrap around your triangle so that the back is completely covered and the sides are covered top to bottom 2/3" of the way to the point of your triangle. If necessary, re-roll your scraps to obtain enough clay sheet for this.

"I don't think I will ever tire of this," declared Peele, as she industriously pinched and stretched the clay with her fingers. "It is such a marvel to see how these patterns get smaller and smaller with each inch they lengthen—yet lose nothing of their integrity!"

"Yes," replied Parker, working on her own cane. "But I do wish I could just roll the silly thing to stretch it—however, therein lies disaster, I know too well."

Step 3: Reduce the canes and reassemble

Working slowly and carefully, reduce this triangle until it is 7 1/2" (See Primer —Reducing) in length; cut this long cane into 6 1 ¼" pieces.

Reassemble the six pieces, matching the sides as well as possible, and reduce this new cane until it is 5" long. Cut into four equal pieces.(About 1 1/4" each).

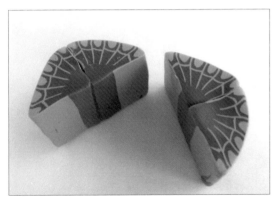

Press one pair together, and reshape on the work surface into a half circle, outer color on the outside.

Repeat with the other pair.

Using a tool, press a channel along the center of each of these half-circles and insert a 1/8"snake of the outer color. Assemble the halves into a whole circle.

Sheet the remaining outer color to a medium thin thickness (About 2 playing cards) and wrap the entire log, leaving the ends exposed.

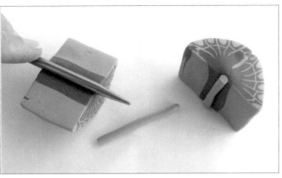

Reduce this cane into a snake just larger than ¼ inch. Don't worry about making it perfectly even along the length, as slight variations in size add to the realistic look.

Cut the snake into 8 equal pieces and reassemble into your final cane, making sure to press together well to avoid or remove any air pockets.

Let rest for at least an hour.

For examples of how the other color formulas will produce different beads, please see illustration on the next page.

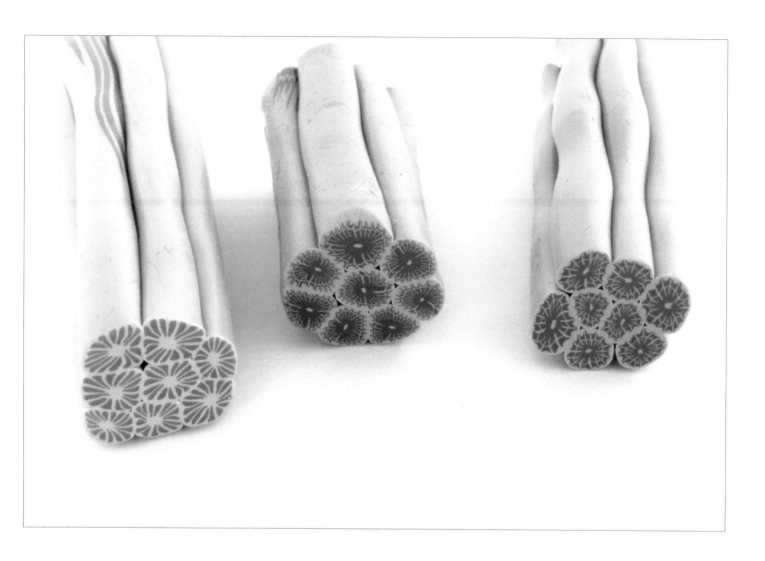

"Look at this!" cried Parker, waving her completed cane under her companion's nose, "Was there ever a prettier pattern?!"

"Indubitably;" replied Peele. "I have it just here."

My Dear Apprentice

    There is a fine art to illusion, and this necklace which we are about to create is a perfect example. Though it appears to be massively heavy, it is in fact absurdly light, an effect created with the most commonplace of materials—this new foil made of aluminum, which supplants the older wrapping foils made of tin. Vastly superior, in my estimation.

Supplies:

Aluminum foil

Fossilized coral canes

Bead stringing wire

Fine metal wire (optional)

2 crimp beads

Clasp (choice)

Freshwater pearls (choice)

Metal spacer beads (choice)

Leftover "outer" cane color from making canes

Tools:

Wire cutters

Crimping pliers

Heavy piercing needle

Electric Drill and bits

Rock Hound Necklace

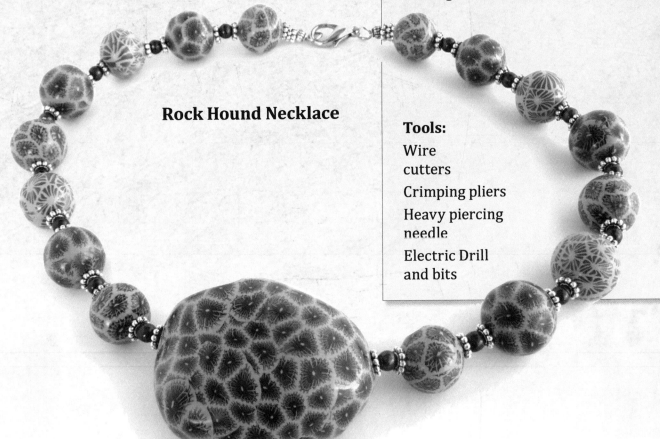

Step 1: Create the focal bead

Begin by shaping an armature out of aluminum foil. This creates a large, lightweight bead. Tear off a one foot square of foil. Roll it into a loose ball and then shape into a stone shape about 2" by 1 1/2".

Pierce through the long side of the scrunched up aluminum bead core, about 3/4 of the way up the bead (not through the center) and enlarge the hole a bit. Cover with a layer of scrap clay, rolled to a medium-thin setting on the pasta machine (about 2 playing cards, See Primer—Sheeting.)

Cover the holes one at a time, coming back through from the other side to open the hole through the clay layer. Smooth the scrap clay with your acrylic roller.

Choose the cane you wish to use, if you have made several different colors, and use thin slices to cover the bead by placing them side by side.

Use partial slices to fill in bare spots.

Smooth them on to the surface using the acrylic roller. Make sure that you keep the holes open as you did when covering the bead with scrap clay.

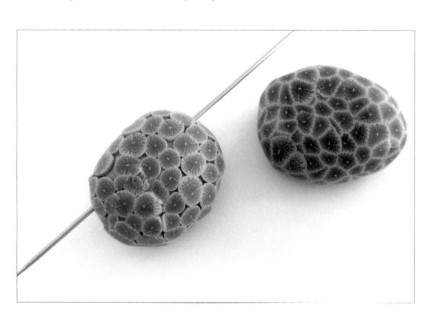

"What are you doing, dear gel?"

"Oh," said Parker modestly, "I just ran a bit of thick wire through the bead to keep track of the holes whilst I am covering and smoothing it."

Peele raised an eyebrow. "Wish I'd thought of that" she muttered.

Step 2: Make the additional beads.

For the round beads, gather up the scraps from the canes. Roll into a log, ½ inch in diameter. Cut the log into ½ inch pieces. Roll each piece into a round shape. Cover with thin slices of the cane. If you have made several canes, make beads of each, about 6 or 7 from each cane.

Don't worry if the slices are uneven or if there are bare spots. Overlap slices or tear them to fill in a spot. The more irregular the cane slices are, the more natural the beads will look. Roll between your palms until they are smooth and any lines have disappeared.

Depending on the size of your beads (this necklace functions best as a choker) make enough for your desired length. Cure at the recommended temperature for at least 30 minutes for the solid beads, but less time for the focal, as the clay layer over the foil is thin. (See Primer —Curing). Let cool.

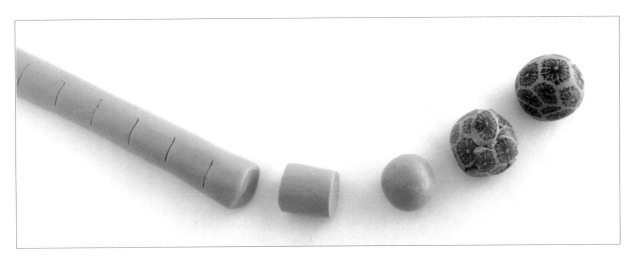

"Hhmmm," said Peele. "I see it's time to use that accordion folded paper again—bloody beads roll everywhere."

Step 3: Finishing the beads.

When the focal bead is cool, use a contrasting color and fill in the stringing holes. Cure at the normal temperature for ten minutes. This will keep the bead from taking on water during the sanding process. When the focal bead is sanded and polished, drill out the contrasting color.

Sand and polish all beads This is one that really benefits from being buffed on an electric buffing wheel. If that is not available, you may wish to use a finish such as Renaissance Wax.

Step 4: Stringing the necklace

Cut a strand of beading wire or other stringing material about 6 inches longer than you would like your necklace to be.

String the focal bead. (You may find it helpful to create a 'needle' from a piece of fine wire bent in half to pull the stringing material though the focal—the aluminum foil core sometimes 'catches' the stringing material and stops it from going through) Working from the center out, string a spacer, a pearl, then another spacer.

To make the necklace as illustrated, add a round bead to each side, then a spacer, a pearl, and a spacer. Continue this pattern until necklace reaches desired length, remembering to vary the different bead patterns.

String on your crimp, pass through one side of the clasp, back through the crimp, and back through the last bead.

Tighten the crimp using your crimping pliers, and trim the excess stringing material.

"Well, old bean," declared Peele, turning this way and that to admire her reflection; "this is a proper conundrum, this is; looks substantial enough to cosh a horse, but weighs no more than a silk scarf. I daresay we'll turn a few heads at dinner tonight."

the Secret of the Ammolite

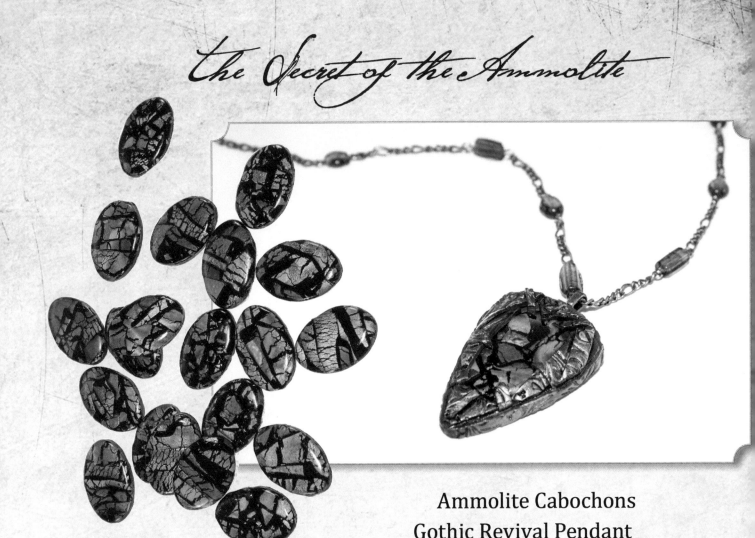

Ammolite Cabochons
Gothic Revival Pendant

My Dear Apprentice

Like the previous lesson on Fossil Coral, here we venture into the realm of the antediluvian. Ammolites are the fossil remains of great cephalopods who swam the natal seas, enormous tentacled creatures whose shells recall the nautilus , though their descendants are in fact the humble cuttlefish. Eons in the earth transmuted them into astoundingly iridescent gems. I first came across them in my Canadian travels and vowed to reproduce them; I have succeeded beyond my dreams.

Step 1: Sheet and color the clay

Condition your black clay (See Primer—conditioning) and sheet the full blocks to a medium thickness on the pasta machine (3 playing cards; See Primer—sheeting), one sheet per block. Lay one sheet aside. Leave the remaining half block for later. Cut the first sheet in half, and lay the pieces on deli sheets or plastic wrap for ease of handling. Use the dropper in the ink bottles to randomly deposit ink drops. On one sheet, drops of Hot Mama Red, Volcano Red, Sundown Magenta and Mazuma Gold. On the other sheet, Galactic Blue, Macaw Green, Hot Cool Yellow and Mazuma Gold.

Keep the sheets level, and use your finger to gently join the drops to each other, just enough to form a solid surface. Do not over mix! Add the appropriate ink where necessary for a thick coat with discernible areas of color; if one color is overwhelmed, add it to the surface. Place the sheets in a draft free area overnight to allow the ink to dry completely. It must be dry enough to crack when the sheet is stretched.

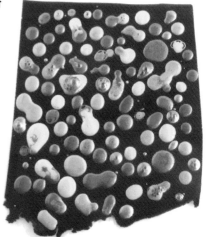

Supplies:

2 1/2 blocks Premo! Black clay

Daler Rowney Pearlescent inks in the following colors: Galactic Blue, Macaw Green, Hot Mama Red, Volcano Red, Sundown Magenta, Hot Cool Yellow, and Mazuma Gold.

Kato Clear Medium

Tools:

Basic tool kit for polymer clay (See Primer—Basic tool kit)

Plastic Deli paper or plastic wrap

Cutter shapes (choice, as illustrated 1.25" oval cutter)

Flexible blade

Heat gun

Soft brush (optional)

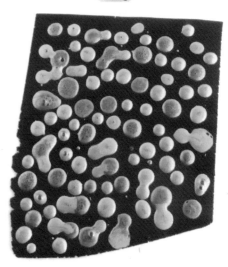

Step 2: Create the effect

When the inks are completely dry, run each colored sheet through the pasta machine on a medium setting, first in one direction, and then another. Step the machine down one setting to medium-thin (2 playing cards) and repeat this process. If the sheet is too wide, trim to fit. Observe the amount of crackle. The amount shown here is slight with larger areas of color. If you desire finer grain, you may step the machine down one setting thinner and run the sheet again.

Run the second black (un-inked) sheet through the pasta machine on a medium-thin setting. Lay your crackled sheet onto it, and trim the edges. This is your 'backing' sheet. Cover with deli paper and brayer the inked sheet down firmly; the pressing action should create more crackle. Gather the scrap, sheet medium-thin and apply the other inked sheet. Gather all remaining black scrap (add to it from the remaining 1/2 block if necessary) and roll a sheet of clay on a medium-thin setting approximately the size of the inked sheets. This is the base sheet. Set the base sheet on a piece of waxed or deli paper for the assembly.

Step 3: Assembling the pattern

You now have two inked sheets in different color schemes, one warm, one cool. Choose one, and cut random strips and shapes; lay these on the base sheet spaced apart, until you are satisfied as to the placement.

Cut random strips and shapes from the other colored sheet, and lay these pieces in between the others, so that you have a variety of colors and patterns.

Overlap and fill in where necessary.
If some areas are too black, patch them with colored bits.

Contrast, however, is good. You will have some colored sheet left over—do not feel obliged to use it all up at once.

When satisfied, lay a piece of deli paper or plastic wrap over the surface, and brayer the surface very smooth. This will cause further crackling and distortion. Several gentle passes are better than firm pressure all at once.

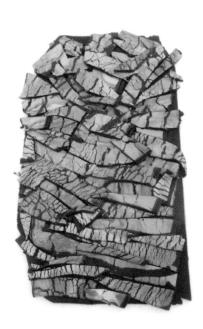

Step 4: Cutting the cabochons

Lay a piece of plastic wrap or candy paper (plastic deli wrap) on the surface of your sheet.

Using your chosen cutter, cut out the shapes, pressing all the way through the plastic to the bottom; cutting through the plastic will both cut your shapes and round the edges at the same time —the goal is flat-topped cabochons with soft rounded edges.

Smooth the cut edges with your fingers if necessary.

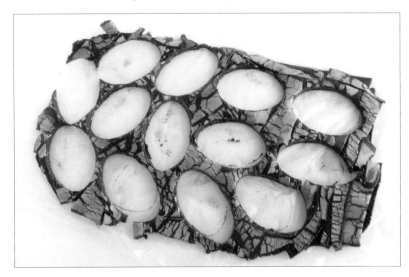

Cut as many cabs as you can, then cut apart the scrap and reassemble into another sheet.

Brayer smooth as before, and cut more cabs; repeat this process as many times as you can, keeping in mind that the final cab can be asymmetrical.

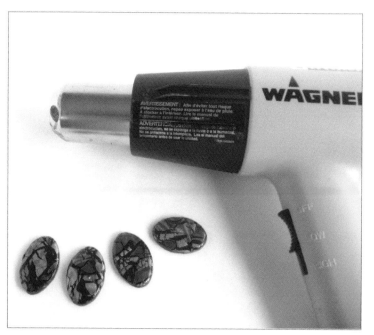

Step 5: Curing and doming

Cure all cabs at the recommended temperature for 20 minutes and let cool.

Apply Kato Clear Medium to each cab in a layer thick enough to cover it completely. Pool the Clear Medium in the center and draw it to the edges with a brush or other tool.

Turn the oven up to 300 degrees, and cure the cabs again for another 20 minutes or until clear. Upon removing from the oven, blast briefly with the heat gun until absolutely clear, taking care not to scorch by moving the heat gun constantly.

NOTE: this process creates irritating smoke—work in a very well ventilated area and observe commonsense precautions, such as using a mask.

Allow to cool, then apply a second, thinner coat of the Clear Medium and repeat curing and blasting. Let cool.

My Dear Apprentice

The somber and beautiful buildings of the Maritimes inspired this lovely pendant, rich in color and antiquity. And what better setting for the precious gem of the North?

Peele sat up straight and made a pleased feline sound.

"What is it, Peele?" asked Parker, looking over her friend's shoulder at the volume in her lap.

"A clue—tiny, but significant." Parker scratched her head. "I'm afraid it has escaped me, "she admitted. Peele grinned. "We'll track it down; "c'est rien."

Supplies:

Finished cabochon

1/2 block Premo! Bronze or Copper clay

Glaze (Future recommended)

Copper metal powder (Mona Lisa recommended)

Copper or bronze glue-on bail

Jeweler's glue or epoxy

24" copper or bronze chain (choice) with clasp

20-30 copper colored headpins at least 2" OR 20 ga. copper wire

Glass beads (choice)

Black acrylic paint

Good quality metallic gold paint (Liquitex Iridescent Rich Gold as illustrated)

Rub N Buff blue patina (or gilder's paste, turquoise acrylic paint)

Deli paper or index card

Liquid clay or Poly Paste

Tools:

Basic tools for polymer clay (including a sharp flexible blade)

Texture sheet (choice, as illustrated, Lisa Pavelka Fancy Checks)

Soft brush

Jeweler's pliers; side cutter, round nose, chain nose and flat jaw

Cutter of the same size and shape as for the cabochons

Gothic Revival Pendant

Step 1: Create the bezel

Condition and sheet your clay to a medium thickness. (3 playing cards; See Primer—conditioning, sheeting) Using the same shape and size cutter as for your cabochons, cut out a shape in the clay.

Place your cabochon into the vacancy, and use a blade to cut the outer shape of your pendant, slightly larger than you wish the finished piece to be.

Gather the scrap and sheet it to a medium thin thickness (2 playing cards) and texture it heavily.

Working on a sheet of deli paper or index card, flip the sheet texture side down, and apply a small amount of liquid clay to the area intended for the cab and setting.

Place the cab and bezel on the sheet and press firmly to adhere. Trim the edges to fit.

Parker cackled with delight, "I say , Peele, this grey texture sheet is the perfect thickness to roll through the machine, and what a pattern it creates on the clay!"

Peele looked up in irritation, "Confound it , you might have mentioned that before I spent all this time trying to roll the texture evenly with this blasted brayer!"

"Well," said her chastened companion, "it did take a moment to realize I had to re-set the machine back to the thickest setting before both clay and texture sheet would go through."

Step 2: Decorate the bezel

Gather the scraps and sheet to the same medium thin thickness and texture as before. Cut thin strips and shapes from this sheet, working in pairs for symmetry, and experiment with overlapping patterns around the cabochon. Do not be concerned with perfect fit—the sides will be trimmed once more.

When you are pleased with the effect, trim all the edges even. Use a very sharp flexible blade, cutting down through all the layers of clay into the final shape.

Dust the setting generously with copper powder (except for the sides), cleaning off any powder which strays to the cabochon with a damp brush or Q-tip. Cure at the recommended temperature for 30 minutes and cool.

Apply a small amount of liquid clay to the sides of the setting. Cut strips from the texture sheet to fit the sides. Apply the strips to the sides pressing gently to retain the pattern and trim at the points. Smooth the seams if necessary, dust with copper powder, and cure for 20 minutes. Let cool.

Step 3: Antiquing and finishing the pendant

This pendant will be antiqued multiple times. Begin by applying a light coat of glaze to protect the metal finish and let dry.

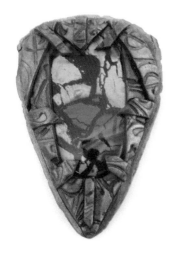

The first coat is a light black wash; dilute the black acrylic paint with a little water, and brush all over the setting. Remove from the high areas with a damp tissue or clean finger. Let dry.

The second coat is gold metallic paint, applied in some but not all areas, again removing from the high surfaces. Gauge the effect. If too bright, more black wash may be applied over the gold. Let dry.

The third coat is the blue patina. This should be applied with the pad of a finger and only to the high areas of the setting. Let dry.

Finish with another coat of glaze and let dry. Apply the glue-on bail, following the manufacturer's recommendations for the type of glue you are using.

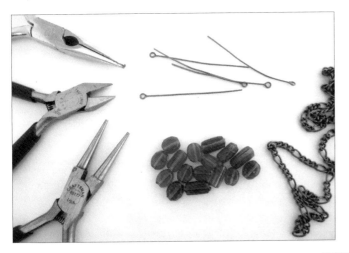

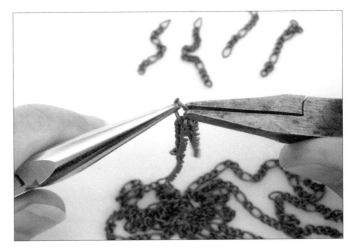

Step 4: Create the jeweled chain

Determine the length of chain you wish. (It can be adjusted as you go.)

Separate the chain into roughly 1" segments. This can be accomplished by cutting with the side cutters, or more economically (as most base metal chain is unsoldered) by opening the links in the following manner:

Grasp one side of the link with a pair of chain or flat nose pliers, and use a second pair of pliers to twist the link open sideways; then twist the link back to close it. Create enough small segments to make up the length of your chain, accounting for the jeweled spacers and clasp.

Determine your pattern of beads, and begin by stringing one onto an eye pin. Make a 90 degree bend in the wire at the end where it emerges. Cut this end to 1/4" or less.

Using the round nose pliers, grasp the very end of this wire at the diameter desired (round nose pliers are graduated to create several sizes of jump rings) and begin rolling it toward the bead.

Keep the jaw of the round nose pliers within the circle as it forms, but release at intervals and re-grasp the wire a little farther back.

This insures a well-centered jump ring as the circle completes. Try to insure little or no gap by adjusting the circle until it closes completely.

When you have created enough jeweled spacers, attached them to the segments of chain by opening the rings on the spacers (sideways) as before.

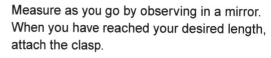

Measure as you go by observing in a mirror. When you have reached your desired length, attach the clasp.

To string the pendant, simply find the center of your jeweled chain, and open the loop on the nearest spacer, slip the chain through the loop, attach and reclose.

"This really is quite lovely," smiled Parker, stroking the chain on her neck. "Do you remember that trip we took to Labrador and Newfoundland? Reminds me of the Gothic Cathedral."

" Yes." replied Peele grimly." I know."

the Bog Oak Horror

Victorian Mourning Brooch

My Dear Apprentice—

The great queen across the water mourned her lost prince for the remainder of her days, and in so doing, created not only a fashion but an industry—the manufacture of jewelry from the ancient trees sunk deep in the bogs of Erin. After thousands of years in the Cimmerian peat, wood becomes hard as stone, and perfectly suitable for the black jewels which the royal grief demanded. It is perfectly easy to imitate with the wonderful medium we have at hand.

Step 1: Create the bog oak cane.

Mix the following quantities of clay (the process of mixing will sufficiently condition the clay):

1/4 block black with 1/4 block translucent (translucent black)

1/4 block black with 1/4 block Alizarin Crimson (crimson black)

1/4block alizarin crimson with 1/4 block translucent (translucent crimson)

Condition the remaining 1/2 blocks of black and translucent. Sheet all the color mixes in 3 inch strips to a medium thickness (See Primer—sheeting) and sheet the black and translucent until they are twice as long as the color mixes. Stack all of the sheets in the following order:

pure black—translucent crimson—pure translucent—crimson black—pure black—translucent black—pure translucent.

Supplies:

1 block Premo! Black

1/2 block Premo! Alizarin Crimson

1 block Premo! Translucent

Findings for brooch—pin back or combination brooch/pendant.

Faceted or cabochon glass or stones (choice) that will fit into a 1.5" oval shape with room for other elements.

Tools:

Basic tools for polymer clay (See Primer)

1.75" Oval cutter

Texture sheet (choice)

Cut the stack into 2" pieces and stack them on each other to form a loaf 3" long and 2" wide. Reduce this loaf lengthwise until it is 8-9" long. (See primer—reducing)

Cut this stack into three pieces with all lines parallel and restack. Reduce as before, cut into three pieces, stack and reduce again to 6".

Cut in half and check to see that the lines are just barely visible. If so, rotate the stacks to 'mirror' each other, compress into a tidy rectangle, and rest until cool. .

Step 2: construct the brooch elements
(unless otherwise instructed, work on an index card for the following steps)

In any design, use your common sense—choose the central point and work outwards for the best possible harmony.

Decide on your focal element (glass or stone). Cut a thick slice (between 1/8 and 1/4") from the cane, roll it on the second thickest setting of the pasta machine, texture it as desired, and cut an oval for your base . Cut another slice from the cane and roll it into a ball slightly larger than your focal element. Flatten this ball until it is deep enough to contain the element, and press the element

deeply into it into it, stopping just short of the bottom. Press the clay evenly and tightly around the element to contain it securely—at least halfway up the sides. Use your blade to cut away on all sides and corners until you form a smooth even bezel around the element—see Illustrations. Use a very thin needle to press lines into the top edges of the bezel to imitate the effect of gallery wire if you choose.

Set this element into the center of the oval and press down securely. From another thick slice of the cane, cut small strips which can be rolled into 6 evenly sized balls about 1/4" in diameter; form these balls into teardrops. Flatten very slightly and use a blade or needle to impress 2-3 lines in each teardrop. Place these around the focal in an even spacing.

Peele heaved a heavy sigh, "Blast it Nosie, I can't seem to get three evenly spaced lines on these bloody teardrops—"

"Silly old sausage," chuckled Parker, "just do the center one first, then put the others on either side."

Roll smaller balls from the cane slices and place these between the teardrops. Roll even smaller balls and place these around the bezel between the ends of the teardrops.

Cut strips from the cane and roll into thin snakes, double them and twist into 'braided' ropes.

Apply one all around the base of the brooch, using your blade to snug it up to the sides.

Cut the other braided rope about 2" long, and form a loop in the center.

Bevel the ends to fit snugly against the oval and attach these to the sides of the brooch as shown.

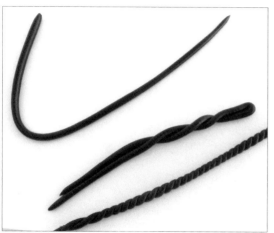

Cut 4 more smaller braided ropes (about 3/4") to run from the brooch base to the end of the braided loop —you may need to adjust the lengths as you go. Attach these securely by gently pressing with a tool.

Cure at the recommended temperature for 20 minutes. (You will be doing multiple curings).

Once cool, form two more teardrops small enough to fit into the ends on the braided loops, and adhere them with a small amount of liquid clay. Cure for 10 minutes.

When cool check all the elements for complete adhesion. If any seem loose, apply small amounts of liquid clay to the base and cure again for ten minutes.

Step3: Apply the brooch back

Cut a slice at least 1/4" thick from your cane and roll this on a medium thin setting (2 playing cards) into a sheet large enough to cover the entire back of your brooch.

Texture roughly to resemble wood—coarse sandpaper or stair tread is excellent. Apply a thin coating of liquid clay to the brooch back, and laying the textured sheet face down, position the brooch on the sheet as desired.

Use your x acto knife to carefully cut all around the perimeter of the brooch. Turn over and smooth all the edges with your fingers or tools, then texture it to blend. Position your pin back as desired, and cut out an area for the bottom of the pin back to rest in. Remove this strip, set the pin back into the recess, and replace the strip to both hide and secure the mechanism; re-texture if necessary. Check to make sure catch opens fully! Cure for 20 minutes.

Step 4: Finishing

Inspect your brooch carefully for any rough edges and sand if necessary. Apply a light wash of black acrylic paint to antique the pin (See Primer—antiquing) and when dry, apply a light glaze to highlight elements of your choice (see Primer—glazes), leaving some areas such as the background matte for an authentic look. Dry thoroughly, and admire your work.

Peele consulted her small hand mirror. "I must say Noelia, this brooch is a handsome piece of work—and there must be a thousand variations. It was obviously important to our forger, as she would not part with it. Not a conventional design, and in fact it does remind me of that silver pendant we made last week."

Parker glanced up absently, engrossed in her own brooch. "What's that, Peele?"

"Oh nothing," returned her companion, "merely thinking aloud..."

My Dear Apprentice—

When she made herself Empress of India, Queen Victoria also inaugurated a passion for the following objets d'art: jewels made from the claws of the magnificent Bengal tigers who were the true rulers of that country.

Though the great white hunters maintain they were performing a public service by the slaughter of these regal beasts, I doubt it; I doubt it.

We may console ourselves through our art that no jungle prince will suffer the indignity of having his deadliest weapons worn as trinkets by a society matron.

Faux Tiger Claw
Victorian Raj Brooch

Supplies:

1 block of Premo! White Translucent

1/16 block of Premo! Pearl

Brown acrylic paint

Tools:

Basic tools for polymer clay (See Primer—basic tool kit)

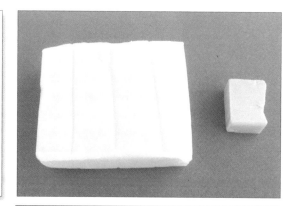

Step 1: Condition the clay

Condition the white translucent and sheet it to a medium setting (3 Playing cards) on the pasta machine (See Primer—conditioning, and sheeting). Condition the pearl clay and roll it into a thin snake the length of the sheet.

Step 2: Create the cane

Place the thin snake of pearl along one long edge of the translucent sheet, and roll the snake up tightly into the sheet. Smooth and compress the resulting log. Reduce this log (See Primer—reducing) until it reaches the length of 12". Fold the log in half, then in half again.

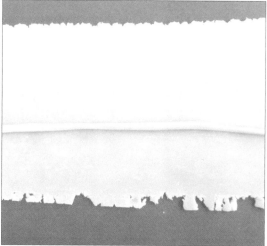

Reduce this thick log by pinching, squeezing and if you wish, by rolling carefully (do not twist) until it reaches the length of 12" again. The seams on the log are a guide—if they are not twisted then neither is the cane.

Fold twice as before, and reduce to the same length again. Repeat this process three more times, or until you observe fine lines of pearl becoming visible in the translucent clay. These lines must be hair-fine in the final log.

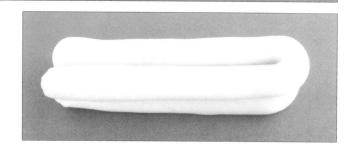

"This is quite amazing," murmured Peele. "That tiny amount of pearl clay is suddenly visible on the surface, after all that fol-de-rol. I never would have imagined."

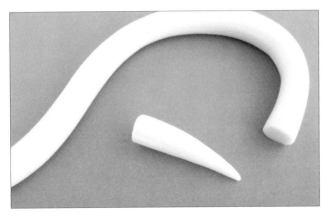

Step 3: Form the claws

Roll your final log smooth until it is a generous half inch in diameter, then cut two pieces 1" in length. Pinch one end into a point, then roll smooth on your work surface.

NOTE: work from this point on with gloves or finger-cots to avoid fingerprints.

Gently twist the piece; the faint pearl lines will turn from horizontal into vertical, like the growth lines of a real claw. Curl into a realistic shape.

Working on an index card, shape by pressing on the lower (inside) edge of the blunt end with your finger, elongating and flattening it.

Be careful to leave the pointed tip and upper edge of the claw rounded—this is very important for authenticity. Work solely on the inside edges of the claw—leave the outer rounded edges alone as much as possible.

You may also pinch and 'draw' the inside edges down. Flip the claw over occasionally to work both sides and avoid areas that are too flat.

When satisfied as to shape, smooth away fingerprints (if not using gloves). Check for size; if too long, cut off the blunt ends.

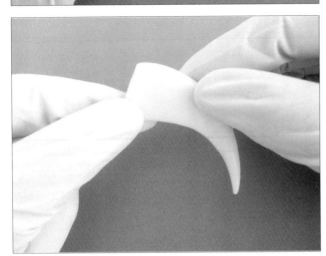

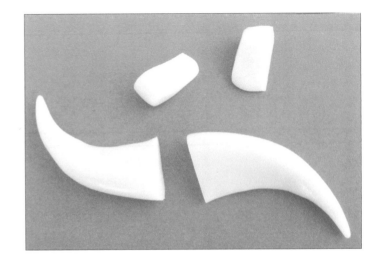

Step 3: Distress the claws

Using your craft or craft knife, draw tiny jagged lines on the sides of the claw near the base, about half way down the flattened area, like fissures and growth lines. Tiny pock marks and divots are also very authentic.

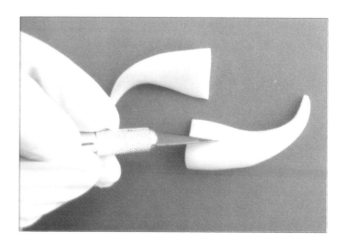

Adjust for shape and smoothness, then adhere the two claws to each other, (if making the brooch as shown) being careful to center each thin edge to the thick edge of the other claw.

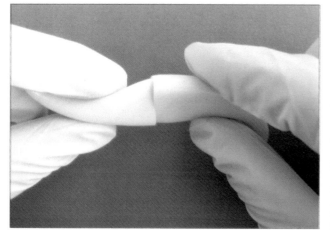

Optionally, you may leave the claws separate for other uses.

Cure at the recommended temperature for at least 45 minutes. (See Primer—curing) Toss into ice water immediately out of the oven to increase translucency.

Step 4: Antique and finish

Sand and polish your claw to a pleasing sheen. Use brown paint to antique the distress marks (See Primer—antiquing) Dry and buff once more to a shine.

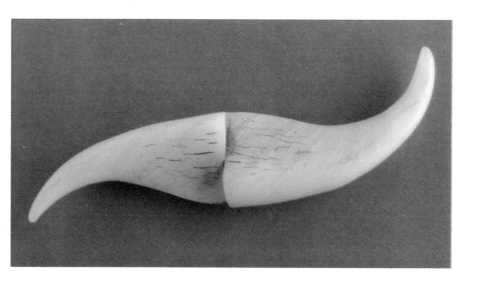

"Oh, Peele," shuddered Parker, holding the wicked claw up to the light. "This looks so real I can't help but imagine myself in the brute's clutches..."

"Dear Nosie," said Peele with a mischievous grin, "not to worry! You're far more likely to be carried off by a mountain lion in these parts."

Victorian Raj Brooch

Step 1: Create the base

Apply liquid clay to the center of the claw assembly at least 1/2" out from the center. Using small amounts of clay, build up on either side of the center to create a level 'platform' ; this will serve as the base of the pin back, and will be covered with a veneer of textured gold clay.

When you have achieved a level surface both the front and back, use a flat clay shaper or other tool to 'true up' the sides. (One way to check for a level surface is to press your claw assembly flat onto an index card; it will show any low areas that need to be filled.)

Check to make sure that the pin back has sufficient support, and press gently into the clay to create a small groove. Remove.

Cure at the recommended temperature for 30 minutes and let cool.

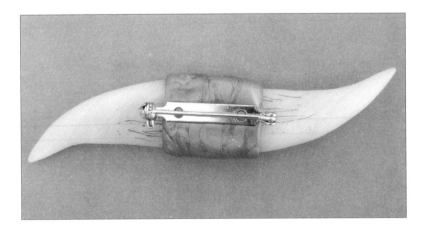

Supplies:

Finished tiger claw assembly

1/2 Block Premo! Gold clay—any shade

1 glass or gemstone jewel (choice)

Brooch back (pin back) at least 1"

Liquid clay

Gold powder

Glaze

Copper paint (as illustrated, Liquitex Iridescent Rich Copper)

Renaissance Wax

Tools:

Basic tool kit (See Primer—Basic tool kit)

Texture sheets or stamps (choice)

Step 2: Cover the base

Sheet a small amount of the gold clay to a medium thin setting. (About 2 playing cards)

Texture this sheet with a decorative stamp or other media.

Cut a strip just long enough and wide enough to cover the base, and after applying liquid clay, place the pin back in position and wrap this strip with the seam to the back, pressing gently to avoid distorting the pattern, and completely covering the base of the pin back.

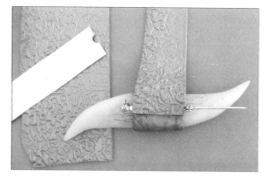

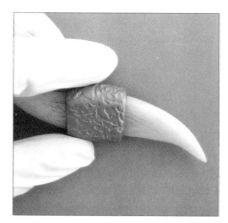

Check to make sure that the pin back is securely fastened. Smooth the sides, re-texture the seam if necessary and generously dust the veneer with gold powder.

Remove any powder that strays to the claw itself with a moist brush.

Cure at the recommended temperature for 20 minutes. Let cool.

Lightly glaze the gold-dusted areas to prevent scuffing on subsequent handling.

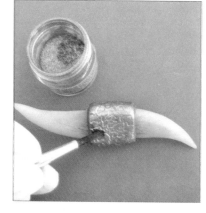

Step 3: Decorate the sides

Roll a thin snake of gold clay, and after applying liquid clay to the sides of the base, apply this snake, again beginning at the pin back.

Smooth and snug this snake to the sides, seating it well to hide the edges of the base.

Use a blade or craft knife to impress a pattern of lines in the snake, then use a ball stylus or knitting needle to press a divot between each line for a decorative pattern.

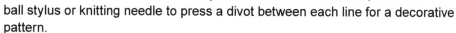

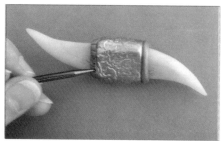

True up the sides if necessary. Dust completely with gold powder and cure for 15 minutes.

"Now I see why this project is cured between all the steps" said Parker.

"What a mess it would have been to try this all at once in the raw clay!"

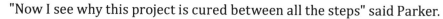

Step 4: Create the gem setting

Roll a ball of gold clay and flatten it into a disk deep enough to hold your chosen gem. Push the gem into the clay, pressing the clay up snugly against the sides to hold it securely, sloping slightly away from the top.

Use a blade to cut away the sides and corners and create a thin bezel. Use a needle tool or blade to impress a pattern of tiny lines on the top edge of the bezel.

Dust thoroughly with gold powder and cure for 20 minutes. Let cool and glaze if desired.

Apply sufficient liquid clay to the base of the gem setting; center the gem on the face of the brooch, clean up any excess liquid clay, and cure for 20 minutes. It is advisable to 'cradle' the brooch in an accordion folded index card or batting.

Step 5: Finishing the brooch

When the brooch is cool, use a coarse brush and good-quality copper metallic paint to antique the visible surfaces; this will give it the look of red gold.

Heat set the paint by returning it to a warm oven for a few moments.

When cool, lightly glaze the gold areas if desired.

Buff the claw areas and apply a coat of Renaissance Wax to them; when dry, buff with a soft cloth to a shine.

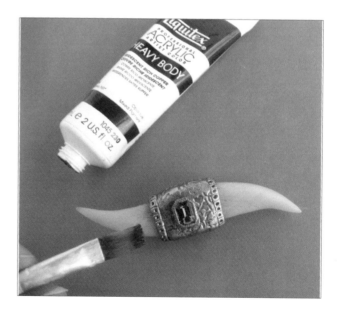

Peele gave a low whistle. "This one, Nosie; this one, I shall wear with exceptional pride. I feel quite sure that no one will ever guess its true nature—and I'm tempted to make up a great tale of foreign potentates and mysterious cases to go with it."

the Favrile Affair

Faux Tiffany Glass Scarabs
Scarab Necklace

My Dear Apprentice

To the great Pharaohs of Egypt, the lowly dung beetle, which I am sure you have observed sturdily rolling its ball through the dust, symbolized the daily journey of the Sun God Ra across the heavens—and by extension, the rebirth of the world every morning. When Mr. Tiffany recently chose to reproduce this creature in his famous favrile glass, it was an instant success.

Step one: Form the scarabs

Condition all of your black clay (see Primer—conditioning) and pinch off enough to roll a small ball about the size of a grape.

Pinch this ball into a teardrop shape, and flatten it slightly on your work surface.

About 1/3 of the way from the narrow end, use your oval cutter to impress a curved line deeply into the clay.

Use the dull side of your straight blade to deeply impress a line above the curve to form a half-round shape.

Use the flat of your blade to press the narrow end of the scarab into a flat shape about half the height of the rest of the scarab. This is the 'head'.

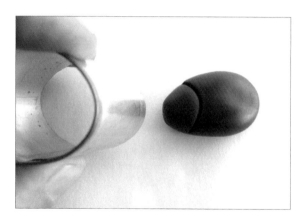

Supplies:

2 blocks Premo! Black

Jacquard Pearl-ex mica powders: Interference gold, True Blue, Blue Russet, Spring Green, Interference Violet

Gold Metal Powder (Mona Lisa Recommended)

Glaze (Future recommended)

Black acrylic paint

Texture sheet (Choice)

Texture sheet in hieroglyph motifs—(optional) in this case, a child's toy (See suppliers)

Tools:

Basic tools (See Primer —Basic tool kit for polymer clay)

X-acto knife

Plastic stir straws

Soft brushes in different sizes

Coarse brush

Oval cutter 1.25"

Cosmetic sponge, wipes, tissues, etc.

Use the dull side of your blade to deeply impress a line down the center of the 'body', being sure to follow the curve and cut all the way to the bottom; rock your blade slightly from side to side to deepen the channel and create a definite notch at the bottom.

Use the dull side of the blade to further impress shallower lines parallel to the deep center line. These are the wings.

Smooth away as many finger prints as possible. Slightly round the flattened area of the head with your fingers and smooth. Using the stir straw, impress a series of tiny circles into the head. These are the 'eyes'. (The order in which these steps are performed is of little consequence, so long as they are all performed.) See the illustration below for an alternate sequence.

Step 2: Coloring the scarab

Using one color at a time in any order but being sure to reserve the Interference Gold for last, 'paint' your scarab, dusting the colors on with your soft brushes and overlapping the colors only slightly. Note that the interference colors are somewhat fugitive, which is why they are applied last.

Work with light coats—it is desirable that some black should show through, and all of the colors are more vibrant on pure black than over each other. When satisfied with the effect, cure at the recommended temperature for 30 minutes and let cool.

Repeat for the other scarabs. The number is up to you, but you will need at least nine for the illustrated necklace.

"Oh," breathed Parker, clasping her hands with delight. "See how this Interference Violet simply glows over the black clay."

"Doesn't it though," agreed Peele. "Painting with these mica powders is just ever so jolly. I've noticed too that the colors are much more striking if they don't overlap too much."

Step 3: Antiquing

Lightly glaze each of your scarabs to protect the finish and let dry completely. Using your coarse brush and black paint, antique each scarab to bring out the contrast (See Primer—antiquing) Wipe off the paint from the high areas. Let dry and re-glaze if desired.

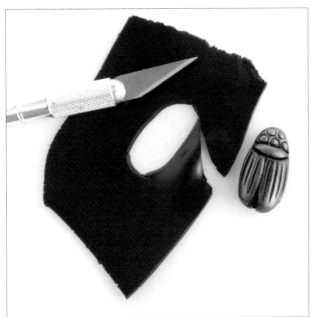

Please note; in this case, black clay covered with gold powder will be used as the bezel, for a more ancient effect; however, you may at your option use gold clay, as in the Faux Metals chapter.'

Step 4: Setting the scarabs

Roll your remaining black clay into a long narrow sheet on a medium thin thickness (About 2 playing cards See Primer—sheeting).

Apply a small amount of liquid clay to the bottom of your cured scarab, place it on the sheet and use your craft knife to cut around the shape of the scarab. Press the raw clay firmly to the cured.

Cut a strip of clay from the sheet no higher than the 'head' of the scarab, and long enough to encase it.

Wrap the base and cut the ends flush, smooth the seam, and smooth it to the clay sheet on the bottom forming a 'bezel' around the scarab.

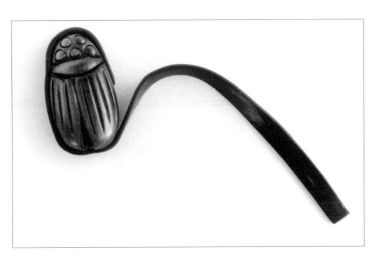

"I say, Nosie," observed Peele, "these clear stamps are

so much easier to work with than those opaque rubber sheets—with small areas like this, I do like to see

what I'm doing."

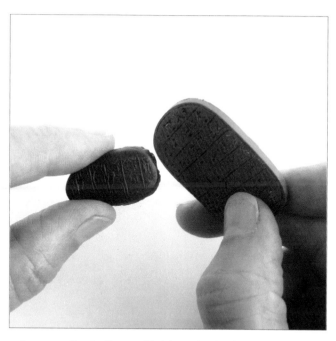

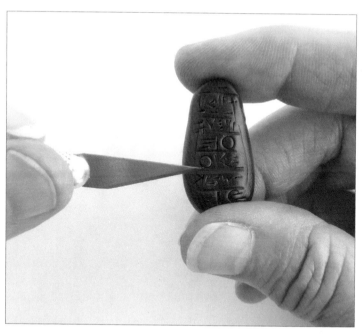

Impress the bottom with hieroglyphs from either a texture sheet, a child's toy, or if you cannot obtain either of those, decorate in the following manner: use your blade to impress a series of parallel lines, then use your craft knife and stir straw to create 'cuneiform' text —triangle, dashes, circles and half circles.

See the illustrations for inspiration.

Color the bezel and bottom with the gold powder, covering thoroughly, and removing any excess from the scarab itself.

Cure for 30 minutes and let cool. Glaze and antique as you did the scarab.

Step 5: spacer elements

Roll your remaining black clay into a thick slab about the height of the bezels. Cut this slab just slightly wider than your longest scarab. Cut into 8 angled strips about 1/4" wide at the bottom.

Use your oval cutter to impress a curved line near the bottom and on the sides as shown.

Use a blade or other tool to create three deep lines below the bottom curve.

Apply the gold metal powder, cure, and when cool glaze and antique as you did the scarabs and their bezels.

Scarab Necklace

Step 1: Determine your pattern

Arrange your scarabs in a pleasing pattern .The necklace illustrated uses 9 scarabs and 8 spacers, but you may use more or less as you choose; if you have one larger than the rest, you may wish to use it as the focal. Also decide which spacer elements go where at this point. You may alternate, as illustrated, or mix up the order to suit yourself.

Step 2: Drill the elements

Using your electric hand drill, drill each of your scarabs horizontally near the top. Check when halfway through to make sure you are drilling straight from all angles. (See Primer—drilling).

Supplies:

9 Finished scarabs

8 Finished spacer elements

Stringing material (choice)

Clasp (choice)

Crimp tubes or beads

Black glass beads (choice), but include both seed and E beads as well

Gold accent beads (choice)

Tools:

Jeweler's pliers, flat jaw or chain nose and side cutters

Electric drill and drill bit the size of the cord you plan to use for stringing.

Step 3: String the elements

Begin at the center of your necklace, and pass your stringing material through the body of the first scarab. Keep in mind that in order to achieve a symmetrical 'hang' for this large flat necklace, you may be obliged to add and subtract spacer beads depending on the variation in your scarabs

Use your E and seed beads as the 'fillers' between the scarabs and the spacers. The look should be 'fanned', with the tops closer than the bottoms, so adjust the number of beads as necessary.

Pull tight after each addition and check the hang in a mirror. When you have strung all of the scarabs and spacers, string the larger black beads you have chosen and alternate these with gold beads for contrast.

The pattern is up to you.

Check in the mirror frequently. When your necklace is just shy of your desired length, slide a crimp onto your cord, pass it through the clasp and back through the crimp, (if possible also through a few beads to hide the cord) and flatten the crimp firmly with the pliers. Trim the cords. Take up all the slack and repeat for the other side.

Now go walk like an Egyptian.

Noelia held up the looking glass and struck a pose: "What do you think, Peele?"

Peele stepped back to consider. "I'd say Cleopatra in all her glory would be outshone," she replied.

My Dear Apprentice

Herein you will find the method for reproducing that luscious creamy Ivory whose trade literally brought nations to their knees; had it not been for ivory, the slave trade might never have existed, and we all know what effect it had upon our young country.

Faux Ivory
Ivory cuff Bracelet

Thanks to the wondrous properties of our medium, no great beasts must sacrifice their lives for human greed. Polymer is exceptionally suited to this task, having all the lovely color and warmth of that once-living material.

Note: In this instance, one must keep the work area as clean as possible. Light colored clay picks up the smallest contaminations. Stop frequently to clean the work surface, or suffer exasperating delays.

Step 1: Mix the colors

Color A:

Condition and roll one block of white translucent, and one block of white to the thickest setting on the pasta machine (9 playing cards). (See Primer—sheeting)

Cut four 3/4" circles of white, and add them along with six drops of butterscotch ink and two drops of slate ink to the translucent white. Mix by rolling through the pasta machine, folding after each pass until the color is uniform.

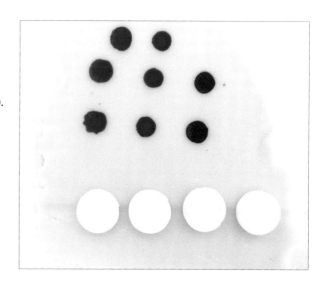

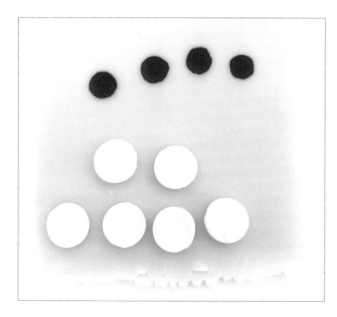

Color B:

Condition and sheet the second block of white translucent as the first. To this add six 3/4" circles of white and four drops of butterscotch ink.

"Nosie," said Peele," have you observed that the color mixes much faster if you give it a quarter turn after folding, before sending it through these infernal machines again?"

"I haven't," replied Parker, "but By Jingo, I'll give it a try."

Supplies

Two blocks Premo! White Translucent

One block Premo! White

Ranger alcohol inks Butterscotch and Slate

Tools:

Basic tool kit (See Primer—Basic tool kit for polymer clay)

Card stock

Plastic wrap or deli paper

3/4" circle cutter

Step 2: Form the block

From the card stock, cut a 3x4" rectangle to use as a work surface and guide, and lay it on your work surface. Cover it with deli paper or plastic wrap so the clay does not stick to it.

Roll Color A through the pasta machine, stepping down one thickness at a time (See Primer—sheeting) until you reach a medium thickness (3 playing cards). Using your card stock template, tear and lay strips of color A lengthwise to fit on the template. Set aside remaining clay.

Roll Color B to a medium thickness on your machine. (3 playing cards) Tear narrow strips off this sheet and layer longwise onto Color A.

You should have an irregular mass of clay strips layered onto your base color (A). Cover this layer of strips with another layer of Color A strips, continuing to add layers, alternating colors, as you build the block.

Press each layer down thoroughly to eliminate air pockets, and re-roll the scraps as needed, keeping the colors separate and the thicknesses the same. Continue until all clay is used up.

Compress the block and even up the edges. Reduce the block along its longest dimension (See Primer—reducing) by rolling with the acrylic roller and gently pulling until is twice the original length, keeping the sides as even as possible. Cut in half and stack, keeping all lines parallel. Compress as before, just enough to smooth the block. Let cool before cutting slices.

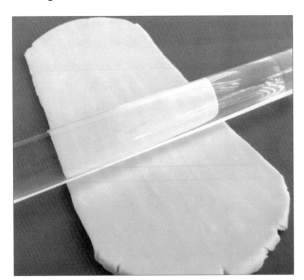

Before starting this piece, make sure that your work surface and hands are impeccably clean.

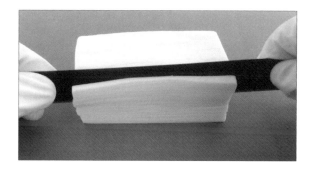

Ivory Cuff Bracelet

Step 1: Cut and sheet slices to apply to the blank

Begin by taking 1/8 inch slices from the block, parallel to the subtle lines of color (the long side).

Starting at the largest setting of the pasta machine, run each slice through the machine with the stripes perpendicular to the rollers.

Turn the handle slowly, to help keep cracks from developing.

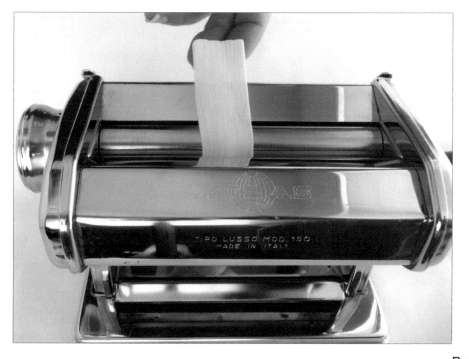

Supplies:

Ivory cane block

2 inch aluminum bracelet blank

Gloves (optional)

Deli paper or index card

Renaissance wax (optional)

Tools:

Acrylic roller

Soft tip clay shaper

Pasta machine

Blade

Run each slice through 2 more times in the same direction, stepping down one setting each time. You will end on a medium setting.

This process insures that no matter how unevenly cut the slices are, they will all end up with the same thickness; this will save some sanding. If the edges of the slices are uneven, trim them straight with the blade.

A note, Dear Apprentice—

You are no doubt wondering why we are refraining from using any type of adhesive medium on the blank. The answer is simple; the blank will be completely encased in clay, and such precautions are unnecessary. What IS necessary is to take care that there are no air bubbles trapped between the clay and the metal so make very sure of this!

Step 2: Apply the slices to the blank

Begin covering the inside of the bracelet with the slices, with the stripes running cross-wise to the length of the bracelet.

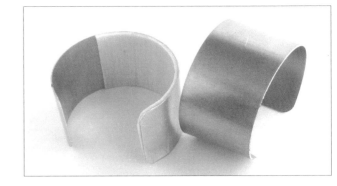

Gloves are recommended while doing this to eliminate fingerprints. Make sure each slice fits as tightly as possible against the next one.

Trim off each slice even with the edge of the bracelet. Using your fingers and the clay shaper smooth the joins between slices. When the inside is completely covered and smoothed repeat the process for the outside of the bracelet. The acrylic roller or clay shaper is very useful to smooth the slices on the outside.

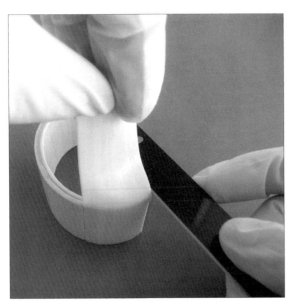

Step 3: Join the inside to the outside.

When you have the slices as smooth as possible, re-trim the edge of the bracelet with your blade.

With thumb and forefinger, gently press the inner and outer layers of clay together to cover the edges of the bracelet as smoothly as possible.

It is helpful to press the bracelet against a clean piece of paper to even up the edges.

Inspect and trim if necessary, smooth and cure for recommended time.

Sand through 2000 grit and polish.

Apply a coat of Renaissance wax, if desired.

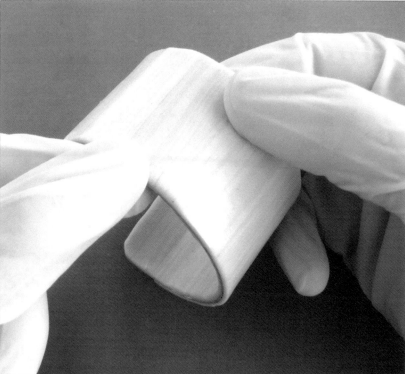

Peele held up her wrist and turned it in the light to admire the perfect sheen of her bracelet. "I believe I shall make another of these," she declared. "It's so easy, and they are perfectly beautiful!"

"True," returned her companion, "but we shall be obliged to explain their origin to all we meet, so that we are not accused of bagging innocent elephants—I'm rather fond of elephants myself."

"Isn't that the best part?" asked Parker, "That this marvelous brummagem could save the lives of hundreds, who might otherwise be slaughtered for their tusks?"

Epilogue

~Some days later~

"I feel an uncommon need for magic this evening," announced Peele, " let's go to the Follies, shall we?" As darkness fell, both were ensconced in front row seats at the venerable Pecan Street theater, libations in hand. Parker noted that Peele kept a firm clutch on her reticule.

Jugglers, comics, and singers plied their arts, until at last The Magnificent Vixens appeared; billed as a sister act, the reclusive magician and her lovely assistant had for the past few years been headliners of the show. As their performance reached a brief pause while stage hands prepared for the finale, Peele slipped a note to a passing usher. The magician opened it, and her color changed remarkably under the heavy stage makeup. She cast a lightning glance around the audience. Peele caught her eye and tilted her head meaningfully in the direction of the exits, which were quietly filling with constables. An icy look passed between them.

"Ah, ladies and gentlemen," the magician announced, after drawing a deep breath, "we now come to the pinnacle of our performance— if you please—" A large and ornate cabinet was wheeled upon the stage, festooned with Mayan glyphs and feathered serpents. "and now," continued the magician, staring directly at Peele, "we require a volunteer; no ,no, ladies and gentlemen, no use throwing up your hands —my assistant will choose." The assistant, a diminutive dark-haired woman, wended her slow way through the crowd, pausing here and there to inspect candidates and pass them by with sad shakes of the head; as she returned to the stage, she suddenly turned and offered her hand to Parker, who accepted it with squeals of delight, over the energetic protests of her friend.

Parker mounted the stage and averred at the magician's request that no, she was not a performer, merely a townsperson, and at her invitation entered the cabinet, which was immediately sealed upon her with much ceremony. Mysterious incantations issued from the magician's lips:

"Rio, frio, brazos, blanco! Llano, llano, estacado!"

Flashes of light and billows of smoke boiled over the stage, and when they cleared it was to reveal the cabinet in ruins, the magician, her assistant , and Parker—all vanished.

Peele made her way back to the Driskill in wretched silence. An exhaustive search of the theater by the police had revealed nothing beyond a few trumpery effects left behind by the absent magician; there was no trace of Parker. As she passed amongst the late night revelers on Sixth Street, she felt a rude tug at her elbow.

A street urchin thrust a note at her. "For you, miss," he piped, and took to his heels before she could stay him. Peele snatched open the note:

A hasty scrawl read simply:
Be at the Pennybacker Bridge at midnight. Come alone.

Peele consulted her watch and flagged down a passing cab. She gave him directions, "Drive like the devil," she cried, and he whipped up his nag at once. Just upon the first stroke of midnight, she arrived at the foot of the old iron bridge spanning the great river whose current divided the city far downstream. A half moon shed a pale light upon two figures waiting in the center of the bridge and Peele recognized the form of the absconded Noelia, blindfolded, bound and gagged beside her captor.

Peele began to advance, and a gesture from the magician stopped her in her tracks. Peele called out: "Mrs. Little Thin Fox, I presume?"

"Full marks," sneered the magician. "You winkled me out—will you do me the courtesy of telling me how you did so?"

Peele leaned upon her bumbershoot. "You were a difficult case, but in the end, it was a question of what didn't belong. That Pueblo-style silver pendant in the first volume—it simply didn't fit. I applied to the Reservation authorities and they informed me that the silversmith who had created the original died some years ago, leaving behind a wife and sister. The description of the wife was lengthy—the daughter of a French Trader, remarkably well educated, with a keen interest in history. Someone who spent a great deal of time in the Gothic Revival buildings that our Northern neighbors love so well. A casual comment about your acquaintance with a Romani magician, as well as the surname Fox, suggested both your line of work and the stage name which concealed your identity. Still, what puzzles me is this—why turn to forgery when you had a lucrative stage career?"

"You are a fool," replied the widow bitterly, "always assuming greed—'twas revenge! Revenge! My dear husband created the first truly unique style of American jewelry, only to have his work dismissed as trinkets by the self-appointed experts; he died of heartbreak, and I was determined to trip up those effete intellectual snobs. I planned to flood the museums and private collections of the world with my forgeries. Having long dabbled in this extraordinary medium I knew its potential well, and when the time was right, I would discredit all them all, and expose them to the scorn they showed to my love. My former career as a stage magician made me much practiced in the arts of deception."

"I can see by your blood-stained hands," murmured Peele under her breath, but aloud she asked, "So what now?"

Mrs. Fox laughed shrilly. "Now," she said, "the silly little Parker will accompany me to the carriage I have waiting at the foot of the bridge, and we shall depart for destinations unknown—my sister-in-law is already fled far beyond your grasp—and when I am assured of my safety, your companion will be released unharmed."

Peele drew her electric torch from her reticule: "Allow me to amend that proposal." She shined it twice at the far end of the old bridge, and the sturdy tramp of boots announced a contingent of constables advancing out of the darkness, hauling along a very uncooperative coachman.

Peele strode forward. "The game is up," she declared sternly. As she drew near, her quarry suddenly pushed Parker into her with a screech "Curse you, Peele!" and swung simian-like to the rail of the bridge. For an instant she teetered, then leapt from the bridge in a graceful swan dive.

The constables rushing up were greeted by a distant wail of "Adieu, monde cruel!" and the echo of a splash.

~Later that week~

"Another cup of tea, Nosie?" asked Peele. Late afternoon sun peered through the curtains of their sitting room.

"Lovely," agreed Parker, handing over her cup. She rubbed her neck with a yawn. "Can't believe almost two days have passed since all this happened; I'm still exhausted. But all's well that ends worse—do the police venture any hopes of recovering the body?"

"None, " replied Peele, settling back into her chair, "that current runs swift and deep all the way to Matagorda Bay. I fear she has given us the eternal slip—and of her accomplice there is no trace; nor have I the heart to pursue if I could. Without the guidance of her mentor or those volumes I do not fear a fresh outbreak, and little enough damage was done; the Baron embarrassed, as he richly deserved. Her husband suffered a great wrong, and perhaps at some future time his surviving work will come into its own."

"One question," begged Parker, putting up a hand. "How the devil did the police get there? My captor swore there was no time between the delivery of

200

the note and midnight."

"In fact there was little," admitted Peele, "but I directed the coachman to go over one street to the corner of Treaty Oak and gave directions to the constable stationed there. He ran to fetch reinforcements."

Parker laughed "Him? He's the slowest man on the force!"

"Ah," returned Peele, "but not under the spur of a double eagle."

"Oh, Peele," muttered Parker, with a pleased blush.

A chime sounded at the door. "No doubt the police," said Peele, rising to answer it.

She opened the door upon the disheveled Nelson, shaking back his braids. "Package for you miss— delivered special by messenger."

Peele returned to the sitting room and stared thoughtfully at the little parcel in her lap.

carnelian bangle

"Who is it from?" asked Parker, craning to see. Peele began unwrapping the string.

"No return address." She opened the box and held up a magnificent mourning brooch.

"How beautiful," breathed Parker, "is it...?"

"Yes," replied Peele somberly. "The last hurrah of our talented adversary."

Parker took and turned it over in her hands, marveling at the craftsmanship. "Even holding it, I would never guess it to be polymer." She said, "It must have been sent before she fled to the bridge."

Peele rubbed her chin thoughtfully as she studied the wrappings. "Oh, aye, possibly," she said slowly, "save for the fact that the paper is still damp..."

Secret Sources and Further Reading

Arnold Grummer
http://arnoldgrummer.com
iridescent glitter

Art Beads
http://www.artbeads.com
beads, findings, metal cuff bracelet blanks

Best Flexible Molds
http://bestflexiblemolds.com
clay molds and tools

Bear Creek Pottery
http://bearcreekpottery.com
tissue blades

Cool Tools
http://cooltools.us
tools, texture sheets

Cake Supply Stores (various)
molds, cutters, modeling tools

The Clay Factory
http://Clayfactory.net
clay supplies, findings, tools

Craft Stores
http://michaels.com
http://joann.com
http://hobbyloby.com
art and clay supplies

Creative Journey Studios
http://creativejourneystudios.com
gilder's paste, Renaissance Wax

Dick Blick
http://dickblick.com
clay/art supplies

Fantasy Beading
http://www.ebay.com/usr/fantasybeading
cuff bracelet blanks

Fire Mountain Gems
http://www.firemountaingems.com
jewelry supplies, beads

Foredom
http://foredom.net
drills, bits and buffers

Harbor Freight
http://harborfreight.com
tools and sanding supplies

Hardware Stores   (various)
tools, parts, and finishes, etc.

Jerry's Artarama
http://jerrysartarama.com
art/clay supplies, Daler-Rowney inks

Metal Clay Supply
http://tools, cutters, and texture sheets

Munro Crafts
http://munrocrafts.com
art/ clay supplies and tools

Neuberg & Neuberg
http:glandmp.com
artist-grade metal powders

One of a Kind Artist Emporium
http:// http://ooakartistemporium.com
iridescent glitters

Polymer Clay Express
http://polymerclayexpress.com
art/clay supplies

Polymer Art Supplies
http://polymerartsupplies.etsy.com ephemera and dichroic films

Rio Grande
http://www.riogrande.com
tools, findings, beads and finishes

Rockler
http://rockler.com
Renaissance Wax, sandpapers

Sun and Moon Craft Kits
http://sunandmooncraftkits.com
jewelry findings

Texas Art Supply
http:// http://www.texasart.com
art/clay supplies

WEBsturant Store
http:// www.webstaurantstore.com
plastic deli sheets (papercon #433cp8)

Donna Kato
Everything she writes

Marie Segal
The Polymer Clay Artist's Guide: A Directory of Mixes, Colors, Textures, Faux Finishes, and Surface Effects

Julie Picarello
Patterns in Polymer

Websites and blogs:

Polymer Clay Daily/Studio Mojo
http://polymerclaydaily.com

Daily Art Muse
http://www.dailyartmuse.com/

The Polyclay Gallery
http://polyclay.com

Clay Lessons
http://www.claylessons.com/

Polymer Clay Central
http://polymerclaycentral.com

IPCA—The International Polymer Clay Guild
http://theipca.org

Glass Attic
http://glassattic.com

Flickr (just search polymer clay)
http://flickr.com

Pinterest (just search polymer clay, but set a timer--you'll need it)
http://pinterest.com

Desired Creations (Desiree McCrory)
http://desiredcreations.com/

Inspirations:

Books we love:

Carol Blackburn
Making Polymer Clay Beads

Irene S. Dean
Faux Surfaces in Polymer Clay

Lindly Haunani/Maggie Maggio
Polymer Clay Color Inspirations

Tory Hughes
Polymer the Chameleon Clay

Kim Schlinke has been making things since she hit the planet. Starting with doll clothes made from her mother's sewing scraps, she has explored many forms of creative expression. Self-taught, she has dabbled in painting, fiber arts (weaving, spinning and knitting), mixed media, woodworking and interior decorating. She earns her daily bread as a Sample Maker and Production Coordinator for local fashion designers

In December of 2002 she received her first pasta machine as a Christmas gift, after seeing Donna Kato work her magic on the Carrol Duval Show. Polymer clay became her passion. The limitless possibilities of the clay drive her continuing discoveries.

Her polymer clay buttons are featured at Gauge Knits and Fabriker, both in Austin, TX.

Kim currently serves as Vice President of the Austin Polymer Clay Guild.

Randee M Ketzel came to polymer clay by way of a youthful career as a bench jeweler; when impending motherhood frowned upon such diversions, she turned to alternative materials, and in decent middle age, discovered—or was discovered by—polymer clay. She has happily immersed herself in its wonders ever since.

She currently lives, breathes, and teaches the exquisite art of polymer clay in Austin TX with her beautiful children, wonderful husband and an impossibly fluffy little dog.

Her work may be viewed on Flickr www.flickr.com/photos/8989180@N02 , and on Etsy, RMKdesign.

Her work has been featured on *Polymer Clay Daily*, in national magazines, Marie Segal's book *The Polymer Clay Artist's Guide* and in art museum stores.

Your Notes & Recipes:

CPSIA information can be obtained
at www.ICGtesting.com
Printed in the USA
LVIW02n2226171113
361683LV00003B/6